ORGANIZATION
IN THE MIND

Tavistock Clinic Series

Margot Waddell (Series Editor)
Published and distributed by Karnac Books

Other titles in the Tavistock Clinic Series

Acquainted with the Night: Psychoanalysis and the Poetic Imagination
Hamish Canham and Carole Satyamurti (editors)

Assessment in Child Psychotherapy
Margaret Rustin and Emanuela Quagliata (editors)

Facing It Out: Clinical Perspectives on Adolescent Disturbance
Robin Anderson and Anna Dartington (editors)

Inside Lives: Psychoanalysis and the Growth of the Personality
Margot Waddell

Internal Landscapes and Foreign Bodies:
Eating Disorders and Other Pathologies
Gianna Williams

Mirror to Nature: Drama, Psychoanalysis, and Society
Margaret Rustin and Michael Rustin

Multiple Voices: Narrative in Systemic Family Psychotherapy
Renos K. Papadopoulos and John Byng-Hall (editors)

Oedipus and the Couple
Francis Grier (editor)

Psychoanalysis and Culture: A Kleinian Perspective
David Bell (editor)

Psychotic States in Children
Margaret Rustin, Maria Rhode, Alex Dubinsky, Hélène Dubinsky (editors)

Reason and Passion: A Celebration of the Work of Hanna Segal
David Bell (editor)

Sent Before My Time: A Child Psychotherapist's View of
Life on a Neonatal Intensive Care Unit
Margaret Cohen

Surviving Space: Papers on Infant Observation
Andrew Briggs (editor)

The Many Faces of Asperger's Syndrome
Maria Rhode and Trudy Klauber (editors)

Therapeutic Care for Refugees: No Place Like Home
Renos K. Papadopoulos (editor)

Understanding Trauma: A Psychoanalytic Approach
Caroline Garland (editor)

Unexpected Gains: Psychotherapy with People with Learning Disabilities
David Simpson and Lynda Miller (editors)

Working Below the Surface: The Emotional Life of Contemporary Organizations
*Clare Huffington, David Armstrong, William Halton, Linda Hoyle
and Jane Pooley (editors)*

Orders

Tel: +44 (0)20 8969 4454; Fax: +44 (0)20 8969 5585
Email: shop@karnacbooks.com
www.karnacbooks.com

ORGANIZATION IN THE MIND

Psychoanalysis, Group Relations, and Organizational Consultancy

OCCASIONAL PAPERS 1989–2003

David Armstrong

Edited by
Robert French

Foreword by
Anton Obholzer

KARNAC
LONDON   NEW YORK

First published in 2005 by
H. Karnac (Books) Ltd.
6 Pembroke Buildings, London NW10 6RE

British Library Cataloguing in Publication Data

A C.I.P. for this book is available from the British Library

ISBN: 1-185575-397-9

10 9 8 7 6 5 4 3 2 1

Edited, designed, and produced by Communication Crafts

Printed in Great Britain by Hobbs the Printers Ltd, Totton, Hampshire

www.karnacbooks.com

For my colleagues at TCS

CONTENTS

SERIES EDITOR'S PREFACE   ix

ACKNOWLEDGEMENTS   xi

EDITOR'S NOTE   xiii

FOREWORD   *Anton Obholzer*   xv

CHAPTER ONE
Organization in the mind:
an introduction   1

CHAPTER TWO
Names, thoughts, and lies:
the relevance of Bion's later writing
for understanding experiences in groups   10

CHAPTER THREE
The "organization-in-the-mind":
reflections on the relation of psychoanalysis
to work with institutions   29

CHAPTER FOUR
The analytic object in organizational work   44

CHAPTER FIVE
The recovery of meaning   55

CHAPTER SIX
"Psychic retreats":
the organizational relevance
of a psychoanalytic formulation   69

CHAPTER SEVEN
Emotions in organizations:
disturbance or intelligence?   90

CHAPTER EIGHT
Keeping on moving   111

CHAPTER NINE
Making present:
reflections on a neglected function of leadership
and its contemporary relevance   124

CHAPTER TEN
The work group revisited:
reflections on the practice and relevance
of group relations   139

REFERENCES   151

INDEX   159

SERIES EDITOR'S PREFACE

This volume traces David Armstrong's enduring preoccupations over the last fifteen years. These preoccupations began even earlier, in the author's work at the Tavistock Institute in the early 1960s. They were sustained during sixteen or so years at The Grubb Institute and came to be re-worked since taking up an appointment in 1994 with the newly formed Tavistock Consultancy Service.

The book is thus rooted in what is now generally known as the "Tavistock approach" or the "Tavistock tradition". And yet the focus is very distinctive. It is not so much centred on the interweaving of the different frames of reference to be found in the varied settings of the work—those of psychoanalysis, of group relations, and of consultancy. The emphasis is, rather, on the deepening and elaborating of the description of phenomena that the author encountered in the course of this work, phenomena that found collective expression in the term "organization-in-the-mind". The originality of the thinking behind this term characterizes this series of brilliant and accessible papers, each bearing on different aspects of the author's subtle and steady efforts to inform the practice of organizational consultancy with, as he says in chapter one, "the insights and methods of psychoanalytic and group relations but [with] its own distinctive integrity as a field of observation".

This is the leading edge of a long-established Tavistock commitment to pioneering the theory and practice of working with groups and institutions. The writing represents the author's own personal endeavour to define and explore the theoretical and clinical foundations of what he calls "the proper object of a psychoanalytic approach to working with organizations". To this end, he revisits some of the conceptual, theoretical, and methodological tools of the trade and demonstrates, through descriptive examples, his close attention to emotional experiences both as the link between psychoanalytic practice, organizational work, and group mentality and as a core ingredient in all mental make-up.

While the work of Wilfred Bion clearly lies at the heart of this collection, the papers also draw on a wide range of conceptual frameworks and of literary and philosophical ideas. Certain well-known terms are revisited and revitalized, freighted with additional significance and energy.

This volume is embedded in work that originated in and was developed by successive thinkers and workers within the Tavistock. It adds a unique texturing to that work, pertaining not only to organizations and group relations but to the understanding of the organization of the human mind. It thus evidences our own conception of the individual, the group, institutions and organizations, and society at large.

Margot Waddell
February 2005

ACKNOWLEDGEMENTS

I am greatly indebted to past and present colleagues at The Grubb Institute and the Tavistock Consultancy Service, who furnished the contexts of experience and reflection within which the papers collected here were written. To W. Gordon Lawrence, I owe both the encouragement and the intellectual stimulus to chart the particular territory these papers set out to explore. To the clients I have worked with, I owe the occasions that set me thinking afresh. Lastly, without the persistence of Robert French, who first suggested bringing these papers together and steered me through the process in the face of very considerable procrastination, the enterprise would have remained still-born.

Four of the papers included were first written for annual symposia mounted by the International Society for the Psychoanalytic Study of Organizations (ISPSO), in London, New York, and Jerusalem. I am especially grateful both for the opportunity and for the challenge afforded by this professional forum.

I am also indebted to Robert Young, as editor of *Free Associations*, who has consistently badgered me into publishing material that might otherwise have languished.

I am grateful to Oxford University Press for permission to reprint chapter five, "The Recovery of Meaning": from R. French & R. Vince (Eds.), *Group Relations, Management, and Organization* (Oxford: Oxford University Press, 1999), pp. 145–154.

EDITOR'S NOTE

Only the Introduction and the brief notes that introduce each chapter have been written specifically for this volume. The rest of the material has already been published elsewhere, though it has undergone some minor alterations in preparation for publication here. The chapters are presented chronologically according to the date of their original presentation. However, this does not represent the "complete works" of David Armstrong. Other published journal articles and book chapters have not been included—either because they do not contribute substantially to the overall theme of the book or because of some duplication of material or ideas. Those who wish to access the work that is not included here should consult the list below.

Other published writings by David Armstrong:

"The Influence of Advanced Technology on the Structure of Management Organizations" (with E. J. Miller). In: J. Streber (Ed.), *Employment Problems of Automation on Advanced Technology: An International Perspective* (London: Macmillan, 1964), pp. 318–331.

"How Do We Help Children Learn from Their Experience in the School Organisation?" In: P. Lang & M. Marland (Eds.), *New*

Directions in Pastoral Care (Oxford: Basil Blackwell, in association with the National Association for Pastoral Care in Education and the Economic and Social Research Council, 1985), pp. 92–99.

"Alienation and Deprivation: The Organisational Perspective." Paper presented at a Social Work Conference, 1990. Available at the Tavistock and Portman NHS Trust Library, the Tavistock Centre, London.

"What Is the Proper Object of a Psychoanalytic Approach to Working with Organisations?" Paper presented at a Scientific Meeting of the Tavistock Centre, 1993. Sound recording available at the Tavistock and Portman NHS Trust Library, the Tavistock Centre, London.

"Thoughts Bound and Thoughts Free." *Group Analysis, 27* (1994): 131–148.

"What Does Consultancy Really Mean?" (with J. Bazalgette & J. Hutton). In: R. Casemore, G. Dyos, A. Eden, K. Kellner, J. McAuley, & S. Moss (Eds.), *What Makes Consultancy Work: Understanding the Dynamics* (London: South Bank University Press, 1994), pp. 185–203.

"Making Absences Present: The Contribution of W. R. Bion to Understanding Unconscious Social Phenomena" (http://www. humannature.com/group/chap3.html), 1995.

"The Psychoanalytic Approach to Institutional Life: Why So Little Impact?" *Group Analysis, 28* (1995): 33–45.

"Co-evolution: A Word in Search of Meaning." Dialogue presented at Matrix on Social Dreaming as Memoirs of the Future, at The Institute of Group Analysis, 1996. Available from the Tavistock Consultancy Service.

"Introduction." In: W. G. Lawrence (Ed.), *Social Dreaming @ Work* (London: Karnac, 1998), pp. xvii-xxi.

"Thinking Aloud: Contributions to Three Dialogues." In: W. G. Lawrence (Ed.), *Social Dreaming @ Work* (London: Karnac, 1998), pp. 91–106.

"Destructiveness and Creativity in Organizational Life: Experiencing the Psychotic Edge" (with W. G. Lawrence). In: P. Bion Talamo, F. Borgogno, & S. A. Mercai (Eds.), *Bion's Legacy to Groups* (London: Karnac, 1998), pp. 53–68.

"What Is the Emotional Cost of Distributed Leadership?" (with C. Huffington & K. James). In: C. Huffington, D. Armstrong, W. Halton, L. Hoyle, & J. Pooley (Eds.), *Working Below the Surface: The Emotional Life of Contemporary Organisations* (London: Karnac, 2004), pp. 67–82.

FOREWORD

Anton Obholzer

Rather as in the travel industry there are "trade secrets", places that only the cognoscenti know about and are loath to share with the public, so access to the work of David Armstrong has, until now, been restricted to those "in the know". Nonetheless, through his work at The Grubb Institute and with the Tavistock Consultancy Service, Armstrong has inspired a generation of young entrants into the field of organizational consultancy. He has also been the intellectual mainstay and stimulant (as well as, at times, a conceptual saddle-burr) for many of his peers. The publication of these "occasional papers" now makes his work available to a much wider audience. It will undoubtedly give further impetus to consultancy approaches that recognize the importance of unconscious factors in the life and destiny of our social and economic institutions.

Over the years many perspectives have been brought to bear on thinking about and improving the functioning or efficiency or profitability of organizations. Many have turned out to be passing fads—the managerial equivalents of the "placebo effect", known so well in the field of health. These fluctuations in fashion have, however, also led to an increasing awareness of the importance of underlying emotional factors in the life of organizations. The various permutations of these emotional elements have an impact at many levels. They not only affect individuals who lead, manage, or work in organizations, but also manifest themselves in groups, institutions, and industries, and as global phenomena. These emotional dimensions of institutional functioning are now recognized to be a key factor in the life—and death, for that matter—of organizations. They are, in a sense, the "last frontier" that needs to be opened up for understanding and insight if we are to cope with the turmoil of the twenty-first century.

The place of emotion in organizational life, its relationship to thinking, and its potential for insight and as a basis for intervention—these have been the core elements of David Armstrong's attention and work. He has used the lens offered by psychoanalytic thinking and practice, particularly the work of Wilfred Bion, to shed fresh light on the dynamics of group and organizational life and on the practice of organizational consultancy. His writings open pathways of understanding that are likely to lead to personal development and creativity in the reader. Unlike many present-day gurus, Armstrong's writing is never prescriptive. Instead, he opens up his thinking processes to the reader and, in so doing, gives us the opportunity to accompany him as he works his way through various levels of thought and insight, from ordinary metaphor to the meta-level of systemic understanding and intervention.

The Tavistock "family of thought" was founded in 1920 by professionals returning from the trenches of the First World War. The core philosophy, which has remained ever since, was of multidisciplinary thought and the cross-fertilization of ideas arising from a wide spectrum of professions and philosophies. This has resulted in a melding of ideas that range from early infant development right through to the study of major global systems and their functioning. The emphasis of this book is on the organizational, systemic quadrant of life, with particular attention to those elements of experience that often remain unspoken and unaddressed, even when they are, at some level, known—"known", that is, in the sense that they are present in emotional experience. Attention to these known but unspoken issues is crucial for our managing the future. In addressing these, Armstrong has undertaken a vital task. He has done so in a way that can be a stimulus and a challenge to anyone engaged in organizational work, whether as leader, manager, professional, consultant, or academic.

February 2005

ORGANIZATION
IN THE MIND

CHAPTER ONE

Organization in the mind:
an introduction

The papers brought together in this book were written over a period of fifteen years from 1989 to the present. They are "occasional" in at least two senses. Each was *written for* a particular occasion—meetings of professional bodies or networks gathered around specific topics or themes, or in response to some invitation to share ideas and experiences. Most were also the *outcome of* an occasion: a moment in consultancy work where a particular line of thought arose or became clearer, or where something read or heard seemed to open up another way of picturing experience or practice.

In preparing them for this publication, I have not attempted to "tidy them up". The papers are presented chronologically, according to the date of their original presentation. The audience addressed is sometimes apparent, sometimes alluded to: there are occasional overlaps and inconsistencies, even contradictions. (Information specific to each presentation is given briefly at the start of each chapter.) In this regard, the book can be read as offering an account of a particular period of "work in progress"—warts and all.

Despite the variety of occasions represented, each paper in different ways derives from and gives expression to a central

1

preoccupation during this period: namely, with exploring and puzzling over the links between psychoanalysis, group relations, and experiences of organizational life, as presented within a consultant/client relation.

The background of experience and practice on which this preoccupation draws is that of an organizational consultant trained within what might loosely be termed the (or a) "Tavistock tradition", as developed by the founding members of the Tavistock Institute following the Second World War (Trist & Murray, 1990). This "tradition" seeks to bring together insights from psychoanalysis, group relations (as developed in the pioneering studies of Wilfred Bion, pre- and post-1945), and open systems theory, to understand and address organizational dilemmas, challenges, and discontents, as presented by individual role-holders, teams, or whole organizations. Recently it has come to be referred to as "system psychodynamics" (Gould, Stapley, & Stein, 2001; Neumann, 1999).

Although originating at the Tavistock Institute, this perspective on organizational life has informed a wide body of practice and thought, both elsewhere in the United Kingdom and overseas. I first encountered it as a junior project officer at the Tavistock Institute in the early 1960s, but it was not until the late 1970s, when I joined the staff of The Grubb Institute, that I began to appreciate something of its potential scope in the practice of consultancy. The earlier papers collected here date from the last few years I spent at the Grubb prior to 1994, when I returned to the "Tavistock" to join a newly established Consultancy Service within the Tavistock Clinic.

Given this tradition and body of work, one might reasonably wonder why the continuing puzzle over the nature of the links between the different elements identified. It is not so easy to answer this question. Partly, it derived from some discomfort over the nature of the evidence drawn on in the engagement with clients. In psychoanalytic practice this evidence is immediate and in some sense transparent: disclosed within the evolution of transference and countertransference processes. The "object", as it were, is there in the room. But in working with, say, an individual executive during a role consultation, in what sense is the "object" there; or, to put this another way, just what is the "object" you are seeking to work with? Or again, suppose you are aware of a particular emotional undertow in that exchange, within what boundary is this undertow to be located?

Similarly, if you are working with a team or group and become aware of the presence of one or other "basic assumption" or dynamic, what is the boundary in relation to which you might offer an interpretation?

Too often, it sometimes seemed to me, one could get drawn into one of two dubious moves: either interpreting at a distance and on the basis of second-hand information (a kind of "applied psychoanalysis"); or interpreting in the "here-and-now" but without reference to the context that defined the nature and purpose of the interaction: understanding something about the organization and/or the clients' relatedness to it.

In effect, I think I was searching for some way of imagining and conceptualizing what I was doing that went beyond "integration" (in the sense simply of an interweaving of different frames of reference), something that captured and served to define a single unified arena of observation and analysis.

The first clue came when I began thinking about a concept that was part of the *lingua franca* of my colleagues at The Grubb Institute: "organization-in-the-mind". This term was first introduced, I believe, by the late Pierre Turquet in relation to his experiences as a consultant (he was also a psychoanalyst) during one of the events that typically make up a group relations conference: the "Institutional Event". In this event, the focus is on examining the nature of the relatedness between members and staff within the conference institution as a whole.

In introducing this term, Turquet was seeking to draw attention to the ways in which one might understand members' behaviour in this event, at least in part, as reflecting and being governed by unconscious assumptions, images, and fantasies they held about the conference as an organization. As Edward Shapiro and Wesley Carr were later to expand the point:

> [Any] organization is composed of the diverse fantasies and projections of its members. Everyone who is aware of an organization, whether a member of it or not, has a mental image of how it works. Though these diverse ideas are not often consciously negotiated or agreed upon among the participants,

they exist. In this sense, all institutions exist in the mind, and it is in interaction with these in-the-mind entities that we live. [Shapiro & Carr, 1991, pp. 69–70]

During my time at the Grubb, we came increasingly to make use of this idea in working with clients, both in role consultation and in assignments with working groups and teams. In a subsequent paper, written by Jean Hutton, John Bazalgette, and Bruce Reed shortly after I had left the Institute, the idea is formulated as follows:

"Organisation-in-the-mind" is what the individual perceives in his or her head of how activities and relations are organised, structured and connected internally. It is a model internal to oneself, part of one's inner world, relying upon the inner experiences of my interactions, relations and the activities I engage in, which give rise to images, emotions, values and responses in me, which may consequently be influencing my own management and leadership, positively or adversely. . . . "Organisation-in-the-mind" helps me to look beyond the normative assessments of organisational issues and activity, to become alert to my inner experiences and give richer meaning to what is happening to me and around me. [Hutton, Bazalgette, & Reed, 1997, p. 114]

With this concept in mind, much of the Institute's work in consultancy focused on teasing out both the conscious and the unconscious "mental constructs" that were informing clients' perceptions and behaviour and the ways in which these might illuminate or cloud the more manifest organizational dilemmas and challenges the client was facing and the way in which these were being framed.[1]

At some point—I am not exactly sure when—it began to occur to me that one might re-work this concept, in a way that I felt closer to my actual experience with clients. In the quotations cited above, "organization-in-the-mind" is described as "*a model internal to oneself*, part of one's inner world". Similarly, Shapiro and Carr refer to "the *diverse* fantasies and projections" of individual members. I began to wonder whether these internal models, images, or fantasies, located in the individual, might rather be a response to something more primary that was a property of the organization as a whole, something that was intrinsic to the organization as one socio-psychic field. From this perspective, each individual's internal model or constructs, conscious or unconscious, might perhaps better be seen as a secondary formation, a particular, more or less idiosyncratic, response to a common, shared organizational dynamic.

Similarly, it occurred to me later that one might need to think about processes of projection in organizational settings in a different way, as a response to something elicited *by* the organizational field and not simply imposed *on* it (cf. the distinction between *en*actment and *in*-actment I make use of in chapters six and seven).

I now began to feel that I had, or at least was near to having, what I was looking for—a means of framing a practice of organizational consultancy, informed by the insights and methods of psychoanalysis and group relations but that had its own distinctive integrity as a field of observation.

In March 1993 I was invited to talk about the work I was doing at a Scientific Meeting of the Tavistock Centre. (At the time the Tavistock Institute and the Tavistock Clinic still shared premises, and these meetings were open to all staff.) The paper was entitled, somewhat presumptuously, "What Is the Proper Object of a Psychoanalytic Approach to Working with Organisations?" In the course of this paper, I tried to spell out for the first time what this approach had come to mean in my own practice. This took the form of a series of propositions, "rather dogmatically stated and perhaps in too abstract terms, but which define for me, as best I can, the rudiments of such an approach in the organisational field: its proper object and mode of enquiry" (Armstrong, 1993).

Revisiting these propositions in preparation for this book, it seemed to me that they may still have value in serving to state the position from which many of the following papers were written. Whether or not the latter bear out what is stated must be left to the reader to judge.

Propositions on the proper object of a psychoanalytic approach to working with organizations

1. The proper object of a psychoanalytic approach to working with organizations is attention to and interpretation of emo-

tional experience, in the meeting between a consultant and a client.

2. The client can be an individual, a group, a team, or conceivably the total membership of the organization.

3. Emotional experience is not, or is not just, the property of the individual alone; it is not located in a purely individual space. In work with organizational clients, be they individual members or groups of members, the emotional experience present and presented is always, or always contains, a factor of the emotional experience of the organization as a whole—what passes or passages between the members.

4. The emotional experience of the organization as a whole is a function of the interrelations between task, structure, culture, and context (or environment). Members contribute individually to this experience according to their personality structure. They also contribute anonymously in "basic-assumption" activity. At the same time, you could say they *are contributed to*—that is, there is a resonance in them of the emotional experience of the organization as a bounded entity, both conscious and unconscious.

5. This resonance has a particular register in each member. That register is determined by the position and role that each member takes within the organizational structure as a whole and the boundary that role relates to.

6. No boundary, however, is impermeable. The emotional experiences registered by any one member, identified with regard to position, role, and structural boundary, will always be related to the emotional undertow of transactions across that boundary.

7. To attend to and interpret emotional experience in the meeting between a consultant and a client in organizational settings is therefore to attend to and interpret the "organization-in-the-mind". This is another way of identifying the proper object of a psychoanalytic approach to working with organizations.

8. The "organization-in-the-mind" has to be understood literally and not just metaphorically. It does not (only) refer to the

client's conscious or unconscious mental constructs of the or-ganization: the assumptions he or she makes about aim, task, authority, power, accountability, and so on. It refers also to the emotional resonances, registered and present in the mind of the client. This is the equivalent to Larry Hirschhorn's graphic phrase "the workplace within" (Hirschhorn, 1988).

9. What a psychoanalytic approach to working with organizations does is to disclose and discern the inner world of the organiza-tion in the inner world of the client.

10. This world-within-a-world can appear as a foreign body, as an extension of the individual, or as a term in the relatedness of the individual to his, her, or their context. It can be denied, dis-owned, defended against, and so on.

11. The aim of a psychoanalytic approach to working with organi-zations is to introduce the client to this world-within-a-world.

12. Introducing the client to this world-within-a-world promotes development in the relatedness of the client to the organization.

13. Promoting development in the relatedness of the client to his, her, or their organization *makes a difference*, which may be temporary or lasting, to the inner world of the organization. (This follows from the assumption that every element of an organization has some systemic connection with other ele-ments.)

14. It is a matter of enquiry what kind of organizational interven-tion maximizes this difference—that is, work with individuals, groups, teams, or whatever.

15. The practice of attention to and interpretation of the organiza-tion-in-the-mind takes place within a defined setting. Among the minimal conditions for this setting are:

• Contracted time, space, and frequency.

• An open agenda (no agenda). The client works with what-ever issues, concerns, episodes, incidents, thoughts, feelings, images, and so forth are in his or her mind. Clearly, the client is likely to bring in at the outset particular problems, dilem-mas, challenges that he, she, or they believe they are facing or need to address. These are not ignored, but nor is it assumed that they are more than presenting material.

- Everything that takes place in this setting is seen in relation to the assumption or hypothesis of the experiential reality of the "organization-in-the-mind", as a term in the relatedness of a person-in-role to a system—that is, everything, however personally it is presented, is taken as potential evidence of this reality.

- No interpretation of the (personal) inner world of the client is sought or made.

- The consultant resists pressure from the client to relate to him or her as "expert"—to teach, give advice, and so on. All such pressure is material for attention and interpretation.

16. There is an important—and to my mind not yet very well understood—question about the place of transference and countertransference processes as material for work within this setting. Certainly both are present. But what is transferred onto the consultant needs to be understood always as some aspect of the organization-in-the-mind of the client. This transference may take the form of making the consultant aware of something relating to his or her own "organization-in-the-mind". Similarly with countertransference: what one can transfer on to the client are unresolved or unknown elements in one's own "workplace within".

17. It follows that the practice of a psychoanalytic approach to working with organizations depends on some experience as a "client" oneself. Experience of individual psychoanalysis may or may not be a necessary condition of working with organizations in this way—it cannot be a sufficient condition.

Two notes of caution

I need to add two notes of caution. First, and *pace* the language of the propositions listed above, I am not wanting to claim that the approach I have described is the only adequate way of conceptualizing psychoanalytically informed consultancy. Clearly there are many other approaches (see the partial survey of the field in Kets de Vries, 1991). This is simply the approach one practitioner has arrived at, from within a certain circumscribed tradition of work.[2] Secondly, I am also not wanting to suggest that this method of work is exclusive of other modes of organizational analysis. Not all the work I and my colleagues do would fit at all neatly into this framework, and there may be times when the approach represented in these papers does not appropriately match a client's needs. Moreover, even within the approach I have tried to outline, there will usually come a time when this method is no longer sufficient: when the focus has to shift to a more sustained consideration of structural or strategic realities. (This was what led Elliott Jaques eventually to repudiate his earlier work in the field, though at the expense, in my view, of throwing out the baby with the bathwater: see Jaques, 1995; Kirsner, 2004; see also the partial discussion of Jaques' later position in chapter six.)

These are matters of judgement as much as of one's own preferred ways of working. I hope nonetheless that in what follows I may at least have conveyed something of both the challenge and the potential value of just one, inevitably partial, starting place.

Notes

1. In their later writing, Bruce Reed and his colleagues at The Grubb Institute draw a fine (i.e., subtle) distinction between the organization and the institution in the mind (cf. Hutton, 2000). This is similar to the position taken by Wesley Carr, among others, who distinguishes between "the institution, which is ultimately a complicated set of unconscious constructs in the mind . . . and the organisation [as] that aspect of the institution that invites conscious reflection and handling" (Carr, 1996, p. 50). For my purposes this distinction is not particularly helpful and can get in the way of working through the respects in which conscious and unconscious processes interweave in generating and being generated by emotional experience in organizational settings. In what follows I have chosen to use the term "organization-in-the-mind", mainly to avoid entering this particular debate. When, as in some of the papers, I refer to "institutions" rather than "organizations", I am not, at least consciously, intending to make any similar distinction.

2. Even within this tradition there is a considerable variety of approach. For a more "classical" version than that presented here, see Isabel Menzies Lyth's Freud Memorial Lecture, first given at University College, London in 1986 (Menzies Lyth, 1989).

CHAPTER TWO

Names, thoughts, and lies:
the relevance of Bion's later writing
for understanding experiences
in groups

"Names, Thoughts, and Lies" was originally written to inaugurate a series of invited public seminars mounted by The Grubb Institute in 1989. The intention of the seminars was to review the field of "group relations" and its continuing relevance for understanding organizational behaviour. The paper set out to consider Wilfred Bion's contribution to this field in the light of his later psychoanalytic preoccupations and the ways in which these both complemented and potentially extended the insights of his Experiences in Groups.

Although I was not aware of this at the time, the paper was to herald many of the themes that subsequently preoccupied me: in particular, the conceptualization of emotional experience as the ground of thought and thinking; the problematization of conventional "boundaries" between self and other, internal and external; and the corresponding need to revisit some of the conceptual "tools of the trade", both theoretical and methodological.

Bion didn't think much of *Experiences in Groups* (Bion, 1961). In a letter to one of his children, he comments wryly on its critical reception compared to his later published work: "the one book I couldn't be bothered with even when pressure was put on me 10 years later, has been a continuous success" (Bion, 1985, p. 213).

It is tempting to interpret this in terms of the redirection of Bion's energies and interests, following his second analysis, with Melanie Klein, from group phenomena to the dynamics of individual psychoanalysis. These he was to explore in a unique series of publications from *Learning from Experience* (Bion, 1962) to *Attention and Interpretation* (1970) and the three volumes of psychoanalytic and partly autobiographical dialogues, *A Memoir of the Future* (1991).

This view, however, ignores the evidence of Bion's continuing interest in and use of the "group" in much of his later writing, including his occasional papers, discussions, and seminars. "A scientific approach to insight in psycho-analysis *and groups*" is, after all, the subtitle of *Attention and Interpretation*.

I believe that it is possible to trace, in his later body of work, lines of thought that complement, modify, and extend the ideas presented in *Experiences in Groups* and that the relative neglect of these lines of thought by practitioners in "group relations" contributes to the sense of a self-inflicted theoretical and methodological atrophy which sometimes seems to surround those who work in this field.

Bion at work: a personal recollection

Some twenty-five years ago, I was a member of what I think was the last "study group" taken by Bion in this country, as part of a group relations course spread over three months or so and directed by Ken Rice at the Tavistock Institute.

Looking back, I cannot recall much of the detail of what happened and was said at those meetings. I do retain a strong visual impression of the room in which we met in Devonshire Street, with its high windows and polished floors, and of my fellow members. These included a prison governor, a prison psychologist, a couple of businessmen, a journalist, a young social worker, and an equally young myself. (At the time I was a project officer at the Tavistock, working on action research projects, mainly in industrial settings.) They were somewhat torrid days at the Tavistock. The Institute had recently split into two factions, headed respectively by Eric Trist and Ken Rice. I belonged to Eric Trist's faction and was only allowed to attend the course at all because Bion was going to take a group. Of Bion himself I remember mostly the persona: his way of walking into the room and sitting down, the evenness of his speech, his air of intense, dispassionate curiosity.

Barry Palmer (1986a) has written of the frequent disjunction between the matter and the manner of consultants' interventions in group relations settings. He suggests that all interpretation is simultaneously a performative or "illocutionary" utterance, and that the group members' response to interpretation is always a compound of response to the content and to the conscious and unconscious performative undertow. That describes pretty accurately my own experience in taking groups and observing others taking them. Doubtless it can be understood in terms of the reciprocal dynamics of transference and countertransference phenomena. But it does not describe my experience of being in a group with Bion. I am not sure what does. It had something of the quality of being faced with what might be called a "pure culture of enquiry". It was extraordinarily unsettling and, in retrospect, extraordinarily moving.

I shall pick up this theme again in a moment. But first I want to comment on two other, partly related, memories. The first, which I was very aware of at the time, as were some other group members, is that Bion never gave the slightest impression of being the author of *Experiences in Groups*. Some of us had read this beforehand with varying degrees of understanding and frustration. We were primed to spot "basic assumptions" at work and to be offered the evidence from our experience of their reality. We were to be sadly disappointed and then intrigued. Nothing Bion said seemed to connect to this bit of conceptual apparatus, whereas in the intergroup events run over two weekends by Ken Rice, Isabel

Menzies, Bob Gosling, Pearl King, and, I think, Pierre Turquet, dependence, pairing, and fight–flight were everywhere—and I think genuinely—to be found.

Bion's preoccupation was elsewhere. But where? In the early sessions he often spoke about "naming" and the use of names: the way naming has an illusory quality, as if it were felt to be the answer to a question rather than the question for which an answer needs to be sought.

"I'm David Armstrong" seeks to identify a boundary around an entity that is myself; to use the language of Bion's later writing, it serves to bind a constant conjunction with a name, which Bion refers to as a definitory hypothesis. But this binding can also be used to restrict enquiry. A boundary for exploration (who is David Armstrong? what is he? where is he here-and-now?) becomes a barrier for defending: this is "me", that is "not me". A limit is set; the unknown is robbed of its power to disturb. The revenge of the unknown is that one can be left feeling curiously empty, unable to make contact with the group, or even with oneself, in any way that has the ring of something authentic (see Bion, 1976a).

In later sessions, a recurring theme was knowledge and the fear of knowledge expressed in rules, morals, and judgements. The meetings of the group took place at the time of the notorious Profumo affair.[1] I recall Bion's bafflement (maybe that's too strong a word) at the moral energy this released in the group, as if we could not entertain the thought that this affair, like the affairs that sometimes surface in group relations conferences, could be under-stood—to adapt a phrase of Clausewitz about war and diplo-macy—simply as the pursuit of politics by other means. Morality was the lie invented to conceal a thought, there for the finding.

Naming, knowing, inventing lies, finding thoughts: these are recurring themes throughout Bion's later writing. I wish to suggest that they are as fertile a ground for exploration in the field of the group as they are in that of the individual. More than that, I also believe that these two fields provide, in Bion's phrase, a "binocular vision" for exploring and understanding the ground of human knowing and un-knowing, becoming and be-ing, without which we are prisoners of our fears and terrors, in both our private and our public lives.

The group as an arena for transformations

Before exploring this further, I want to return to what I said earlier about the quality or tone of Bion's interventions. Often in group relations events you are very well aware when an "interpretation" is being made by the consultant. It is as if somehow it carried the label of "interpretation": in its syntax, complexity, or mode of address. If you are the consultant yourself, you are similarly often aware that this is what you are up to and that the members are aware that you are aware that that is what you are up to. Bion's interventions did not announce their intentions in this way. Was it an interpretation he was offering, or an observation, or a comment, or an opinion? You could not say. It was more like an element from a conversation, without exactly being conversational.

Years ago, I went once or twice to hear the philosopher John Wisdom lecture on "Other Minds" at Cambridge. They were very strange performances. They started out like a lecture, in a familiar way. Then there would be a long silence. Wisdom would gaze at a corner of the room or to the back of the hall and apparently pluck an image or example out of that space, as if it were physically present to him at that instant. He would begin to describe it—a pink elephant, a blue moon, an uneasy spirit. We all shuffled uneasily, suppressing giggles.

Wisdom was as self-absorbed as many great philosophers probably were or are. The links he saw and made in that room were links in a mental space projected in front of him. Because we did not inhabit that space ourselves, we could not make the links, could not see the thoughts he found in the air around him and us.

Bion was not self-absorbed like that, in a space that other people just seemed to inhabit. The links he saw and made were links in a mental space not projected in front of him so much as taken inside him, a space to which the individual members of the group and the group as a whole all contributed. But there was the same sense of being in the presence of a finder of thoughts, offered as food for thought.

Perhaps this style of working is inimitable. But even if it is, I think it contains or exemplifies an important conception about groups, more specifically about the idea of the "work group" (Bion, 1961). Bion is sometimes accused of not taking the "work

group" seriously or of taking it for granted, as sometimes psychoanalysts are accused of taking "reality" for granted, so as to be able
to dispense with it and get on with the "real" business of studying
the various stratagems of evasion and denial. I believe this is
fundamentally wrong and that in Bion's way of working one can
discover a meaning for the work group, in a way that transcends
any simple notion of accommodation to reality and offers a radi-
cally different view of the group—that is, as an *arena for transformations*.

The object of transformation

If the group is potentially an arena for transformations, what is it
that is being transformed, what does the process of transformation
involve, and what is its value?

The first of these questions—what is it that is being transformed—is perhaps the easiest to answer. For Bion, the origin of
transformation—the thing-in-itself (ultimate reality or "O"), which
cannot be known except through the process of transformation—is
always the same. It is *emotional experience*. In his later writing, Bion
is bold or foolhardy enough to claim that all human thought and
endeavour, whatever the field, originates in the transformation of
emotional experience. If one thinks of a painting, a song, a poem,
a novel, even perhaps a piece of pottery, it is not difficult to conceive of this as the artist's attempt to formulate, make present,
and communicate—through colour and line, through sequences of
tones or of words, through the shape and texture of clay—an
emotional experience present to him or her.

It is important, though, for what I shall say later, to make the
point that this act of making present is not (for Bion) an act of
simple representation. Representation suggests a model of something to be represented and something through which it is represented, as if the painter confronted an emotional experience as he
confronts his model: a landscape, a sitter.[2] Making present is not
like this, because, unlike a sensuous object, an emotional experience cannot be seen, tasted, smelled, touched. It is a mental event:
an unknown "x" or thing-in-itself. The only access we have to it is
through the transformations we make or perform from it.

In *The Satanic Verses*, Salman Rushdie writes that the poet's work is "to name the unnameable, to point at frauds, to take sides, start arguments, shake the world and stop it from going to sleep" (Rushdie, 1989). Perhaps there is something a bit megalomaniac about that; also something rather uncanny and prescient. But that first phrase, "to name the unnameable", is, I think, a good-enough description of what is involved in making present an emotional experience—provided, of course, we acknowledge that the name and the thing named are not the same.

When I look at a great painting, say one of Cézanne's still lifes, I do not see the emotional experience that was the origin of Cézanne's transforming work as an artist. Rather, I have an emotional experience *myself* that may lead me to say, "I have never understood that before; how one object reflects and takes up the presence of another." At the extreme, this experience in front of a great work of art may lead me to change my life. I do not just understand or see something new, I *become* something new.

But in claiming that all human thought and endeavour represents a transformation of emotional experience, Bion is going much further than these rather obvious examples. Mathematics, he will say, is a transformation of emotional experience through the language of number; geometry, through the language of spatial coordinates. In some of his later discussions, Bion notes parallels between astronomical discoveries and discoveries in psychoanalysis:

> I am familiar with a psychoanalytic theory of the human mind [presumably his own] which sounds like the astronomical theory of the "black hole"—as far as I can understand astronomical formulation. Why should a psycho-analyst invent a theory to explain a mental phenomenon and, independently, the astronomers elaborate a similar theory about what they think is a black hole in astronomical space? Which is causing which? Is this some peculiarity of the human mind which projects it up into space, or is this something real in space from which derives this idea of space in the mind itself? [Bion, 1974, pp. 61–62/1990, pp. 103–104]

This is a question that it is unprofitable to try to answer. Or to put it another way, the answer is probably both/and: as this 🖐 is my hand and that 🖐 is my hand. The wish to assign priority here is an attempt to resolve a mystery that needs, rather, to be lived with and explored. And this mystery has to do with the connectedness of human realizations of thought, in a particular time and place and in and through the medium of the different sciences or arts, pure and applied.

Bion's way of working and thinking, exemplified here, could be described as fundamentally "*systemic*". He is interested in the way in which there is something in a culture, a context, which reproduces itself in different forms, different realizations, from some common root. And along with this interest goes a deep awareness and concern with the making and finding of *links*: between one person and another, between individual and group, between a word and what it is used to express, between physical and mental, conscious and unconscious.

And in examining these links, experiencing them inside himself in his practice as a psychoanalyst, Bion found himself experiencing again and again a resistance to linking, which at the extreme amounted, he felt, to an attack on mind itself.

Transformations and resistances

Let me quote, again from the late discussions, a reply Bion gave to a psychiatrist who was expressing his puzzlement at an imaginative speculation Bion was offering about the development of personality during intrauterine life:

> My surgical chief, when I was a medical student, was Wilfred Trotter who wrote "The Instincts of the Herd in Peace and War". He drew attention to something which seems to exist. For example, take a group like this: we have a combined wisdom which is extraneous to the little that each one of us knows, but by analogy we are like individual cell bodies in the domain which is bordered by our skins. I think there is something by which this combined wisdom makes itself felt to a great number of people at the same time. We like to think that our ideas are our personal property, but unless we can make our contribution available to the rest of the group there is no chance of mobilizing the collective wisdom of the group which could lead to further progress and development.

There are certain highly intelligent people who cannot stand the perpetual bombardment of thoughts and feelings and ideas which come from all over the place, including from inside themselves. So they cancel their order for the newspapers; they withdraw their number from the telephone book; they draw the blinds and try as far as possible to achieve the kind of situation in which they are free from further impact. So the community loses the contribution that individual can make and the individual mentally dies—in the same way that certain cells in the body necrose.

The body has the intelligence to resist an invasion of foreign bodies like bacteria—or even plants, cocci—and mobilizes phagocytes to deal with these invading objects. Is it possible that we can organise ourselves into communities, institutions in order to defend ourselves against the invasion of ideas which come from outer space, and also from inner space? The individual is frightened of even permitting the existence of speculative imaginations of his own; he is afraid of what would happen if anybody else noticed these imaginative speculations and tried to get rid of him on the grounds of his being a disturbing influence. [Bion, 1980, p. 29]

This reply contains in miniature the core of Bion's highly paradoxical view of groups and experiences in groups. From it I want to draw out three implications:

First, the reply makes it clear that, for Bion, individual and group are necessary for the progress and development of each. It is not just that if an individual's ideas are to enter the public domain they need a group that can contain and work with them, without destroying or robbing them of their vitality, their power to disturb, and without itself being destroyed in the process. The group also potentially embodies a collective wisdom, a multiplicity of resources, centres of awareness, that can feed, add to, fill out what any individual has been able to discern and communicate. This is what I have in mind in talking of the group as an arena for transformations.

But, *second,* this reply also makes it clear that the group, organized as a community or an institution, resists the very opportunities for transformation which its own resourcefulness provides. Each individual, moreover, shares in this resistance. And Bion implies, I think, that this resistance does not only spring from one's being a *group member*. The resistance in the group resonates with the resistance in the individual, under the guise of protecting something felt as personal, belonging only to oneself: *my* idea, *my* experience, *my* thought.

It is common in group relations conferences or events for the consultant or a group member to draw attention to the use of "we", as a representation of an idea of the group as a monolithic, undifferentiated one. It is somewhat less common for attention to be drawn to the similar use of "I". Yet both uses, "we" and "I", often serve the same purpose, from different ends of the spectrum, as it were: to block further enquiry, to set limits to thinking, to preserve a boundary that is felt to be threatened by intrusions from someone or somewhere else. If an idea, an experience, a thought, a feeling, belongs to *us* or to *me*, then we or I may feel it is at least under our or my control. It is something we or I own, and therefore we or I can disown. But suppose it belongs neither to us nor to me. We or I do not know what it will do, what it will lead to, whether it will burgeon into a saviour or a monster, whether it will give us new life or kill us.

It is this possibility that gives such resonance and durability to the myths of Prometheus, Faust, and Frankenstein, of the Garden of Eden and the Tower of Babel. Nothing is safe from thoughts. Only lies are safe—until thought comes along. Or, to put this in Bion's terms, more exactly, the only thoughts that are safe are the thoughts to which a thinker is *absolutely essential*; and the only thoughts to which a thinker is absolutely essential are *lies*. Hence Bion's felicitous dictum: "Descartes' tacit assumption that thoughts presuppose a thinker is valid only for the lie" (Bion, 1970, p. 103).

What is a lie, a "true lie", which is more than just a manifest deceit? Bion puts it like this: a lie is a formulation known by the initiator to be false but maintained as a barrier against statements that would otherwise lead to a psychological or emotional upheaval (Bion, 1970, p. 97ff). The emotional upheaval against which the lie is mobilized is one of "*catastrophic change*"—that is, a change that threatens the psyche, the person's experience of and valuation of himself, which, as Bion graphically puts it, "outrages his moral system". Such formulations are as familiar in groups and organizations as in the relation of one person to another, or to one's self.

This leads me to the *third* implication of Bion's reply. The source of the paradox that the group like the individual simultaneously provides the opportunity for and the forces of resistance to transformation is to be found in the uncertainty, the doubt, the unknowing, which is the defining characteristic of becoming aware of a thought. Or perhaps it would be better to say, of becoming aware of the emotional experience, which, if we can tolerate the frustration of un-knowing, may provide the ground in which a thought can appear. At the heart of this unknowing, this surrendering to a thought in the air, is the fear of catastrophic change.

Thoughts and the group

What has this to do with understanding our everyday experiences in groups, not just groups in group relations conferences, but *any* group: a society, an organization, a family, a tribe, a voluntary association? Some of the time and in some circumstances, perhaps not much. I think we can often exaggerate the extent to which the work of the world, the work we all do, calls for sustained mental effort, an encounter with the unknown. We can get by on habit, custom, the clever tricks of our trade, our native intelligence and wit, provided that circumstances, externally or internally, don't change too much. We are busy, and profitably busy. We are having to be clever, adaptable, shrewd. We are not necessarily having to think.

But, of course, circumstances do change, inside and outside. An environment friendly to our activities and interests becomes unfriendly. Salman Rushdie writes a book.[3] New leaders, new faces, new ideas are abroad. And we ourselves change. Old customs stale, the habits of intelligence seem threadbare.

In such a vital context, which may arise within a single group or organization but which can also infect a whole society, all the phenomena I have alluded to as the essential paradoxes of group life surface and resurface in a way that forces them on our attention. These phenomena may include the following:

First, there is an awareness of emotional experience in the group, on the part of its members separately and corporately, that is unfocused and inchoate. It may not be possible to put this awareness into words, and it may betray itself rather in behaviour and the phenomena that psychoanalysts refer to as "acting out". This experience may be compounded of feelings of excitement, expectancy, despair, loss of control, or emptiness.

A model for illuminating this state, Bion suggests, is the phenomenon of birth:

> I suspect that there is some counterpart of the term "birth of an idea"; that there is some reason to imagine that these painful experiences which we have are related to the process of giving birth to an idea—or "struggling to make a connection", which is an instance of thinking. An institution, a society of human beings may be unable to survive the birth pangs of an idea—it splits apart. We are undoubtedly careless with our psychological midwifery. We seem to feel that the thing to do with a newborn idea is to give it a good hard smack. [Bion, 1980, p. 73]

Sometimes a client approaches us from an organization, apparently knowing *exactly* what the problem is or *exactly* what they want to know, or *exactly* what they want you to do about it, which often involves doing something for, to, or with somebody or somebodies else. It is as if all they require is that someone else takes on a particular job they do not feel their organization is competent enough to do on its own. Their interest is in employing you as a technician, exploiting your expertise. There may be all sorts of other motivations or considerations also, which may need to be sorted out before any decision to proceed is taken. A client who knows exactly what the problem is or what he or she wants you to do about it isn't in the realm of "thoughts" and probably isn't going to welcome it if *you* are. He or she is more likely to be looking for confirmation of ideas that are already know, or handy techniques or tricks to achieve what he or she wants to achieve.

As one explores the situation with the client, one may begin to feel that one is in the territory I have referred to earlier as the "lie"—that is, the statement of the "problem" is known to be unsatisfactory or false but is held to because not to do so would bring about some upheaval, in the organization as a whole or in the client's own perception of his or her role. What happens then will depend on the judgement the consultant makes about his or her capacity and that of the client to confront and work with this possibility.

But a client may also come who seems quite uncertain what the real problem is; who tells a story that leaves you feeling just as confused and chaotic as he or she, who is experiencing a sense of frustration, of the loss of signposts, of turbulence within the organization and outside. Such a client, in the terms I am using, is announcing that he or she may be in the presence of the "unborn idea": something waiting to be formulated in the act of exploration and interpretation between you.[4]

Second, the unfocused awareness of emotional experience in the group (or a representative of the group) is accompanied and may be concealed by other elements, which resist it. An example of this is the assertion or reassertion of boundaries as barriers, either around the individual or the group, through the use of naming as a defence. I have referred to this earlier, in talking about the ways in which the pronouns "I" and "we" can be deployed to prevent recognition of the fact that the new experience is precisely an experience that puts in question the meaning to be given to these "names". "I", "we" have not been here before. Openness to the emotional experience present here and now means being open to the evolution of "I", "we", and the relatedness between them. The insistent use of "I"/"we" betrays the presence of the "not-I"/"not-we" that is already inside me/inside us, waiting to be born.

Such a defensive use of naming can surface in many other forms. For example, my colleagues and myself at The Grubb Institute have been involved in a good deal of work with schools, in particular with groups of senior staff. Schools are organizations currently facing great turbulence both within and without. This turbulence is not only to do with continuous government interference and legislation. There is also an awareness of something in society which challenges and raises questions about the meaning in our present environment of schools, of education, and of training, teaching, and learning. In our experience, many teachers in many schools have the courage to face this turbulence—to experience the uncertainty inside themselves and their institutions and to work with it. But there are also times when the countervailing tendency is very powerful. This often emerges in a defensive preoccupation with and use of *values,* or in the assertion of a certain conception of the teaching profession which is designed to circumscribe what can and cannot be entertained as a thought. "Values" and "profession" are referred to as if they were names whose meaning is already known and determined, rather than hypotheses whose meaning here and now is always open to exploration and evolution.

There is a link between this defensive use of names and the lie (in the technical sense in which I have tried to deploy it). Both will often share, overtly or covertly, a preoccupation with *morality:* what ought or ought not to be, as against what is and is not.

A colleague at The Grubb Institute, John Bazalgette, tells a lovely story of a little girl who was asked to write a short review of a book on penguins. What she wrote was: "This book tells me more about penguins than I want to know." It is the fear that one may learn, or may already have learned, "more than one wants to know" that contributes so powerfully to the lie. Behind this fear lurks a primitive belief that the only good news is *no* news, or at least yesterday's news. And behind this fear, Bion suggests, is persecutory guilt—the idea that fuels the concept of original sin.

In the last volume of his psychoanalytic autobiography Bion refers to guilt, through the mouth of "PA", as:

> One of the fundamentals, one of the basic assumptions. . . . The crime (rational, logical) and the feeling of guilt are natural partners. It is a matter to which justice, morals, intellectual ingenuity can be devoted for so long as anyone can spare the time and energy. [Bion, 1979, pp. 54 & 117]

I do not know whether in using the term "basic assumption" here, Bion intended it to have the associations surrounding its technical use in *Experiences in Groups*. As far as I know, no one has explored this possibility in group relations contexts. It is worth considering. If guilt is a basic assumption in group mentality, then perhaps the institution of the law in society can be seen as representing the hiving off of a "specialized work group" to deal on its behalf with the emotions associated with guilt (Palmer, 1986b; Reed, 1982).

The mobilization of basic assumptions

This reference to basic assumptions introduces a *third* set of phenomena through which the essential paradoxes of group life force themselves on our attention—namely, the mobilization of basic-assumption activity: dependence, pairing, and fight–flight.

So far I have said nothing in detail about these assumptions. This is not because I do not think they are important, but because I think this territory is so well explored, so taken for granted, so pervasive—particularly in group relations work—that it can often obscure or draw attention away from other phenomena and foci of enquiry. We need to get both behind and beyond "basic assumptions", to forget about them, in order to be able to rediscover them and make them new, if they are to retain conceptual vitality and relevance.

I do not think it is necessarily correct to say that the basic assumptions are group defences. In *Experiences in Groups*, Bion sees them as inherent in all group activity. They correspond to three of what he has described as "the basic situations to which the basic emotional drives correspond"—that is, "birth, dependence, pairing, and warfare" (Bion, 1970, p. 66). But, in the constellation I am seeking to describe, I do think that the mobilization of basic assumptions, the particular forms they take, and the occasions on which they force themselves on one's attention has a defensive function. They are attempts on the part of the group to put itself beyond the encounter with the unknown, beyond the realm of thought, of names, and of lies: to find a magical solution to the existential dilemma the group and all its members are in.

What I think those of us who work in group relations settings are not always very good at or attuned to is attending to and characterizing that dilemma. Because we believe basic assumptions to be ubiquitous, we are not always careful enough to note *when*, and to consider *why*, they obtrude on our experience.

Re-framing the "work group" as the arena for transformations

I have referred to phenomena within the contexts I am describing which represent ways of resisting or *escaping* from the meeting with the unknown. But there are also phenomena that represent ways of *going to meet* the unknown. And here we are in the territory of work-group activity or functioning. I suspect that practitioners of group relations have not really begun to do more than scratch the surface of these phenomena conceptually, though practice may be in advance of theory. It is all too easy to shelter behind the crude, simple idea of the work group as the group that meets to perform an overt task.

The trouble is that in the contexts I am talking about—the meeting with the unknown—the overt task itself can be problematic. This is why I think it may be useful to think of work-group functioning not only through the concept of overt task and all its various derivatives,[5] but also through the idea I referred to at the beginning, of the work group as an *arena for transformations*. I do not want to claim that this idea corresponds to a clear, observable reality in group functioning. I am using it (in Bion's terms) as a preconception for which a realization may be found, which will give birth to a conception.

But I think one can detect elements of such a reality in the emergence within a group of imagery, of dreams, of myth, and in the capacity for what Barry Palmer and Colin Evans have called "serious play" (Palmer & Evans, 1989). Or in those moments in a group—which may be more present in the groups of everyday life than in the temporary groups we create in group relations conferences—when people are able to associate to others' material without an irritable preoccupation with ownership and without recourse to a prescriptive idea of "relevance".

Transformations in institutions: the essential tension

There is one final strand of Bion's late thinking I wish to comment on. Throughout his life, Bion had a deep suspicion and distrust of institutional life. In a number of his later seminars, he refers to institutions in this way:

> The trouble about all institutions—the Tavistock Institute and every one that we have—is that they are dead, but the people inside them aren't, and the people grow, and something's going to happen. What usually happens is that the institutions (societies, nations, states, and so forth) make laws. The original laws constitute a shell, and then new laws expand that shell. If it were a material prison, you could hope that the prison walls would be elastic in some sort of way. If organizations don't do that, they develop a hard shell, and then expansion can't occur

because the organization has locked itself in. [in Banet, 1976, pp. 277–278]

Organizations lock themselves in when they are unable to entertain the new idea: whether it comes from inside or outside or through the pores of people's sensitivity to the presence of the not-known. But we can easily lose sight of the fact that any new idea requires some host through which it is not only disseminated, but is also made available for use throughout the community or society or group. Ideas are precarious: they do not necessarily emerge fully formed or in a way that is fully understood. They may be the products of genius or of the flashes of genius that all of us are capable of some of the time. They need assimilation, digestion, translation, and the sometimes painful, patient business of reflection, testing, corroboration.

In *Attention and Interpretation* Bion spells out a model of the "institutionalized work group" as essential for the development of the new idea, the work of genius, the mystic. Through the emergence of the function of Establishment, and the consequent elaboration of rules and of training and criteria for qualification, the institutionalized work group enables a psychological and emotional accommodation to be made to the reality that a genius dies, a flash of genius fades. This function provides some safeguard against omnipotence and the tendency to confuse the idea with oneself, as if one owned it rather than serviced it, strove to realize it day by day:

> The fact that the world's work has to be done by ordinary people makes this work of scientification (or vulgarisation, or simplification, or communication or all together) imperative. There are not enough mystics and those that there are must not be wasted. [Bion, 1970, pp. 79–80]

If I could put this point in a more mundane way, it is out of the tension between the new idea and its container—be that a group, an organization, a society, an individual mind (or, indeed, a word, or a form of art)—that development takes place or, conversely, fails to take place. Without that tension, you would produce either nothing or formlessness, splurge.

If transformations beget resistance, they also require it. It is the relation between the two that is productive or destructive: not either on its own. The tension or the paradoxes I have referred to as intrinsic to all experience in groups and their institutionalized forms is what the American philosopher of science Thomas Kuhn has called an *"essential tension"* (Kuhn, 1977).

And this is the last area in which I think those involved in group relations work could learn something from Bion's later thinking—in being alert to the phenomenology of this relation and to the signs of its presence.

In conclusion

When I first set out to prepare this paper, I thought I knew pretty clearly what I wanted to say. I had read much of Bion's work, and lived with it on and off for many years. I had often talked about it with my colleagues at The Grubb Institute and felt I had experienced links between it and my own experience and practice in taking groups and in consultancy and research work.

Faced with a blank sheet of paper, however, my mind took on that blankness, and I felt rather scared: perhaps the emperor had no clothes. I was tempted (and did not enough resist this) to go back over and over again to the texts, the Bion bible, and pinch whatever clothes I found there. Two weeks beforehand, a colleague asked me what the main theme of the lecture was to be. I mumbled something incoherent and felt rather persecuted by being asked. It took an inordinate amount of time to see that "no clothes" was where I must start from. If I could only allow myself to experience the blankness not as a persecution but as a space in which thought already was but not yet realized, then perhaps I would begin to discover what I could say. Perhaps.

This state of mind in the presence of the unthought thought—the no-thing waiting to be discovered and formulated through the elaboration and playing with preverbal and verbal images, with dreams, myths, preconceptions—Bion has referred to, using a phrase of John Keats in a letter to his two brothers, as *"negative capability"*:[6]

> I had not a dispute but a disquisition with Dilke on various subjects; several things dovetailed in my mind & at once it struck me what quality went to form a Man of Achievement

especially in Literature & which Shakespeare possessed so enormously—I mean *Negative Capability*, that is when man is capable of being in uncertainties, Mysteries, doubts without any irritable reaching after fact & reason. [in Forman, 1931, p. 71]

For most of us, this state of mind, which Bion believed was at the heart of the practice of psychoanalytic insight in individuals and groups, is extraordinarily difficult to achieve. But it is always worth trying, even if, as often as not, we will have to be content to tread in others' footsteps.

Notes

First published in *Free Associations, 3* (1992, No. 26): 261–282.

1. John Profumo, the Minister of Defence in Harold Macmillan's Conservative Government, was involved in a complex sexual "scandal", with assumed security implications, which he first denied to the Prime Minister and the House of Commons but later, under pressure, acknowledged.

2. I do not, of course, want to suggest that, for the painter, the landscape or sitter and the emotional experience are separable out—that is, that the experience is, as it were, superimposed on the object. It is always the "experienced object" that is made present, and it is this experienced object that is the "thing-in-itself", the object and origin of transformation.

3. This is an oblique reference to the furore surrounding the publication, shortly before the paper was written, of *The Satanic Verses*, which led to threats being made on Rushdie's life.

4. The differentiation between these two situations is explored further in the first of three dialogues, published in *Social Dreaming @ Work* (Armstrong, 1998), where I draw a distinction between "two kinds of thinking: thinking 1 and thinking 2".

5. For example, the concept of *"primary task"*, defined as that task which a specified purposeful human system must perform at any given time if it is to survive. This concept has proved notoriously tricky to handle, both because of its indeterminate status (normative or descriptive), and because it can easily fail to distinguish between the related but quite distinct phenomena of survival on the one hand and development on the other.

6. On the relevance of negative capability in organizational contexts, see French (2001) and Simpson, French, and Harvey (2002).

CHAPTER THREE

The "organization-in-the-mind": reflections on the relation of psychoanalysis to work with institutions

This paper was initially read in 1991 to one of a series of annual conferences on Psychoanalysis and the Public Sphere, sponsored by the University of East London. Subsequently, I added a postscript (case example 2 below), based on an assignment on which I was working with Jean Hutton, at The Grubb Institute.

Building from the idea of attention to emotional experience as the link between psychoanalytic practice and organizational work, the paper sought to rework the idea of the "organization-in-the-mind" as a working tool in organizational consultancy, drawing on a particular occasion in which I had first sensed the significance of differentiating metaphor and reality.

Hearsay has it that when the Chairman of the Professional Committee of the Tavistock Clinic some while ago read a paper at the Institute of Psychoanalysis on the psychoanalysis of institutions, a distinguished Kleinian analyst tartly observed that there was no such thing—the concept was empty.

At first hearing, one knows what she means. Psychoanalysis is rooted, in its concepts and methods, on what takes place between two people in a consulting-room. It is, one may say, concerned with understanding the emotional experience contained or made present in that room. Its founder's genius lay in realizing that this emotional experience, resonating and amplified through the medium of transference, opened a door to the understanding of the mind. Opening this door promoted development, fundamentally in the inner world of the patient, though also, of course, in that of the analyst her/himself. Melanie Klein's formidable contribution, as I see it, was greatly to enlarge and clarify the concept of the inner world, its contents and relations, as the focus of development. From this point of view, what focuses analytic work, session by session, term after term, is not so much the relation of the patient to external reality as his or her relatedness to psychic reality within.

When one shifts the focus of attention from the pair to the group, or to the institution, or to society (if indeed there is an adequate referent for that term), the conditions that mark out psychoanalysis as a distinctive praxis—I mean a specific conjunction of theory and method rooted in an identifiable arena of observation—seem to evaporate. What one is left with can sometimes appear as little more than an exercise in applied psychoanalysis. And applied psychoanalysis often does seem a suitable candidate for the appellation "empty". Even Freud's forays in this field tend to the wilder shores of speculation. I do not think there is anything necessarily misguided in speculation. But if speculation cannot find a way back to an arena of observable phenomena, it must remain at best a venture in more or less inspired dilettantism.

To put this another way, psychoanalysis is empirically grounded because the arena in which observations are made is immediately present. The object of enquiry and the medium of enquiry are symbiotic. Too often in applied psychoanalysis there is a parasitic relation between the object of enquiry—such as art, religion, politics, or organizational life—and the medium of enquiry—that is, the experience of individual psychoanalysis or the analysed mind. As a result, one or the other—or both—are robbed of their meaning.

Emotional experience and context

What, then, is the arena of observable phenomena that can ground a psychoanalytic approach to the group, organization, society? What is such an approach like? Does it exist at all? And if it does, is "psychoanalytic" an appropriate adjective to describe it?

One answer, or at least partial answer, to these questions is ready to hand within the Kleinian tradition itself. Which is why, at second hearing, the hearsay comment I started with seems strange and strained. This answer derives from Wilfred Bion's pre-analytic explorations of experiences in groups.

Isabel Menzies Lyth has written that Mrs Klein showed little or no interest in this work, which she saw as a diversion from the central analytic task and method. Similarly, Bion himself, once he embarked on his sustained probing of psychoanalytic thought and practice, only occasionally returned to group work—as it were, on holiday. But he never renounced that work. For example, *Attention and Interpretation* (Bion, 1970), perhaps the finest of Bion's later psychoanalytic writings, has the subtitle: *A Scientific Approach to Insight in Psycho-analysis and Groups*. This subtitle would seem to suggest something common to both, while implicitly reserving the term "psychoanalysis" for its original setting: the interactions of the consulting-room.

Within *Attention and Interpretation* and again in *The Dawn of Oblivion* (Bion, 1979), the last volume of his psychoanalytic novel (1991), Bion draws on a group vertex to illuminate mental processes in the individual, as, for example, in the various modes of relation between container and contained. Clearly Bion thought that there was a link between his work with groups and his work with individual patients. What was the nature of this link? It was not, I think, that the former was an application of the latter, any more than vice versa (although the theoretical chapter at the end of *Experiences in Groups*, 1961, written when Bion was deeply immersed in the Kleinian perspective, is something of a hostage to fortune in this respect). Rather, the link lay in Bion's method of work and how he conceived of this method—namely, to go back again to the subtitle of *Attention and Interpretation*, as a "scientific approach to insight".

At the heart of this approach was disciplined attention to the emotional experience that was present and presented in a defined and distinct setting. Emotional experience was the ground of insight as, for Bion, it was the ground for all formulations of thought. *Experiences in Groups* can be read as a series of inspired reflections or musings on the emotional experiences presented to its author in the presence of groups. The formulations that Bion, more tentatively than his followers' practice sometimes suggests, put forward in these papers—about group "mentality", the interrelations of organization, structure, and culture, the distinction between work group and basic-assumption group, and the tripartite differentiation of the latter (dependence, pairing, fight–flight)—are all grounded in these presented emotional experiences.

The point I want to stress here, though, is how very different this world is from the world of the analytic consulting-room. I do not think any of Bion's formulations in *Experiences in Groups* could have been predicted or derived from classical psychoanalytic practice or its so-called applications. There is a tension between emotional experiences in these worlds that seems irreducible. I want to suggest that this irreducibility needs to be valued and given its due, and, furthermore, that it is only by valuing this irreducibility that the conjunction between "psychoanalysis and the public sphere" can be fruitfully explored. At the heart of this conjunction, as I see it, is the link of method: attention to and interpretation of emotional experience.

There are difficulties with the term "emotional experience". One difficulty is this: Ordinarily we tend to locate emotional experience in the individual, as if such experiences were matters of private ownership. I suggest that emotional experience is very rarely located within a purely individual space. The group setting brings into view different constellations of emotional experience and different mechanisms for dealing with these constellations, because in some sense in changing the object of attention it changes the subject as well. Bion's basic assumptions can all be seen as different ways of unconsciously resisting the threat, actual or potential, that this context poses to the boundary around the individual subject. The paradox is that these unconscious resistances or defences themselves annihilate that boundary.

To work analytically in groups—or, I want to suggest, in organizations—is to use one's alertness to the emotional experience presented in such settings as the medium for seeking to understand, formulate, and interpret the relatedness of the individual to the group or the organization. It is understanding that relatedness, I believe, which liberates the energy to discover what working and being in the group or the organization can become.

The "organization-in-the-mind" as a working tool in organizational consultancy

Case example 1:   The school gardener's story

As a necessarily partial attempt to illustrate something of what I mean, I shall take an incident from some work with a client who was the head of a fairly distinguished boarding-school. I met this client in a series of one-to-one, two-hourly consultations, using a method developed by a colleague at The Grubb Institute, Bruce Reed, and known for short as Organizational Role Analysis (Reed, 1976; Reed & Bazalgette, in press). Such consultations are held at fortnightly intervals over a period of four to six months. The material for work is the client's experiences in his or her own working situation: his or her perceptions, feelings, thoughts, images, described behaviour, or interactions with those he or she relates to day by day.

Although the consultations are one-to-one, I do not construe the client simply as an individual but, rather, as a person-in-role within a system, the system being the "organization", seen as "activities with a boundary", in this case a school. Session by session, the client brings in and offers experiences from the working context that are on his or her mind. I seek to understand these experiences as expressing the client's relatedness to the organization, as saying something about the organization-in-his/her-mind. This notion is meant not just metaphorically but literally. That is, I assume the client's experience is an aspect, or a facet, of the emotional experience that is contained within the inner psychic space of the organization and the interactions of its members—the space between.

In psychoanalytic work, as I understand it, everything that takes place in the encounter between analyst and analysand is seen in relation to the transference, the gathering and interpretation of which is the primary task of the analytic session. In a similar way, everything that takes place in these consultations is seen in relation to this assumption of an inner psychic space, which is organizational and not just individual—the "workplace within", to use Larry Hirschhorn's graphic phrase (Hirschhorn, 1988).

On this occasion (the third session with the client), on the way up to the room we met in, we exchanged apparently casual remarks about a storm the previous day. My client referred to the different ways people view the damage that storms cause to the natural environment, depending on whether they live off the land or simply use it for recreation and pleasure. The conversation continued inside the consulting-room, as my client told me a story about a recent interchange with his gardener.

He had met the gardener surveying a beautiful beech tree and saying rather glumly, "It's got to come down. I'll get another to replace it." My client remonstrated with him, pointing out that it was an old tree that made the view and asking whether it really was necessary to chop it down. The gardener persisted. A week later he had felled it and found it to be extensively rotted. Also, once down, a different view opened up. It became possible to think about other changes to the layout of the garden.

Something about this story made me hesitate. I knew that the gardener was also the school gardener and that the head's house was within the school grounds. The theme of continuity and change had been one occasion for the head coming into these sessions from the start. He seemed to be poised between sensing a need for change in order to keep the school alive—that is, not just surviving, but lively, vital—and fear of destroying what was by all accounts a highly successful and predictable enterprise.

The anecdote of the gardener and the tree seemed to me to be a way of formulating more exactly the situation the head believed he faced. Why should he tell it now? I did not know, but thought I would risk mentioning what was going through my mind. The head then said that he had recently been thinking about a possible new organizational structure for the school. The occasion for this was the impending retirement of the Director of Studies, who represented the old guard. Either he could act now or an opportunity would be lost. He had been wondering how to approach this with senior staff, with an incoming Chair of Governors, and with the powerful but reactionary old-boy network, who never wanted or saw the need for anything to change.

The gardener, one might say, had a picture of the garden in mind which was not the same as the owner of the garden. In acting on this picture he took a risk, the risk of believing that if he did so the owner would see something new. The only authority he had for so doing was the authority of one who tended the garden, who had the garden in view rather than the owner. The story might be taken as a way of externalizing and testing the head's own situation, of rehearsing what it might require to take authority as a person-in-role from his position in this school, now.

That is one way of looking at it. But it turned out not to be the only way. When the session was over, I began to think that I had missed something. I had been implicitly treating the story as simply a metaphor for, a clue or probe to, the thought in the mind of the head. But this ignored the fact that the story concerned the wisdom of the gardener, who was the school gardener, not simply the head's gardener as a private individual, just as the head's house and garden were the school's, not his alone. From this point of view, the gardener could be seen as giving a formulation, it seemed to me, to a thought that was there, in the present emotional experience of this school. By appropriating the story as metaphor, by my colluding with, indeed encouraging, this appropriation, the emotional reality of the story in the life of the school was denied.

I then realized that this denial was itself an element in the head's relatedness to the school. That is, he had a tendency to see the school as over and against him rather than as in him—hence a recurring difficulty he was experiencing in sharing with others the "thoughts" formulated in his mind. He experienced himself as *in* the school but not *of* the school, whereas the emotional reality was that the school was *in* him but not *of* him.

His apparent dilemma as head, which he also interpreted as a personal dilemma—should I leave or should I stay?—was, I felt, a dilemma of the school as a whole, or, to put it another way, the emotional experience of the school contained this dilemma as one of its factors. To be free to work creatively as head of the school meant to be able to formulate this dilemma, given to him by the gardener, as the *thought that was there*, and to find a way not of solving this dilemma himself but of giving it back to the school in a way that might liberate emotional energy in others, not in himself alone: energy to realize thought.

To realize thought, I suggest, is to receive, to formulate (give expression to), and to give back something that is there, which is not of oneself alone, is not bounded by one's own physical or mental skin. It is a mental process that stands over and against a more familiar model of thought as made, as an object of ownership: "my" thought, "your" thought, "our" thought.

From this point of view, one can circle back to and in turn mitigate what I said earlier about the irreducibility of emotional experience in the worlds of individual analysis and work with groups or organizations. Each can be seen as a different, distinct arena for the realization of "thoughts". Thoughts emerge from a matrix of emotional experience. But there is no one such matrix. And each matrix—of the individual, the pair, the group, the organization, the society—is, in turn, probably characterized by a distinctive patterning and variety of resistances and defences. We should not be surprised, therefore, that experience of psychoanalysis does not invariably seem to lead to effective collaboration in organizational arenas. Nor should we expect that psychoanalytic insight will alone resolve or reduce the tensions of social life. There is no privileged arena for the hard slog of insight, because there is no privileged arena for emotional experience itself. There are only the arenas there are, and the practice of insight in each.

It is the practice that links.

Case example 2:   Letting go—a community in transition

For some years, I have been engaged with a colleague at The Grubb Institute on an assignment with a community working with emotionally disturbed and damaged children and young people. The community has a long and distinguished history as a residential establishment. In recent years it has witnessed significant change, both externally and internally. The population of young children entering the community has shifted towards more seriously disturbed and damaged individuals, almost all of whom are now on 52-weeks-a-year care orders. Many are likely to spend all or most of their childhood within this community and will receive all or most of their education in the community's own school. The proportion of older children will be higher. Some are likely to remain there throughout their adolescent years and beyond.

The external context of the community has also changed in other ways. Contractual relations with local authorities have been and will be further influenced by the provisions of a new Children Act and by the growing trend to purchaser/provider models of service delivery. As with other human services at present, there is simultaneously a squeeze on resources and a growing public preoccupation with what happens in residential institutions, particularly around evidence of malpractice, abuse, neglect, and incompetence.

Internally and in part as a response to these external factors, there has been a variety of structural changes: in the deployment of space and of people and in management posts and responsibilities. These structural changes have also been informed by a considered intention to enhance the autonomy and responsibility of the team managers, who head up and lead the individual units or houses. Autonomy and responsibility are wished for from both sides, but may also be seen, overtly and perhaps covertly, as a potential threat to the integrity of the community as a whole and to its underlying ethos, both therapeutic and emotional or "spiritual".

We were invited to submit proposals for working with the community at reviewing its current management structures and practice in the light of the various challenges and opportunities it was facing, and to make recommendations. Our own practice of consultancy is, however, to resist being placed as outside experts who come in, interview people, scrutinize documentation, and then offer some organizational blueprint. Rather, it is to work with the organization and its management and leadership at understanding and analysing their working experience, in a way that can release and enable decision and action to be generated from within.

This model of consultancy was, not without some reservations, worked through and negotiated with representatives of the council of the community, with the two directors and with other members of senior management. As a first step, we began working with the directors using the method of organizational role analysis. The idea was subsequently to move out from this base to a broader pattern of work with other individuals and groups, including members of council, senior managers, the team or unit managers, and the community's panel of consultants. Each phase would be concluded by a summary position paper, discussed with a small steering committee, on the basis of which plans for the following phase would be finalized and agreed.

My colleague and I each worked individually with one of the two directors for four 2-hour sessions, spread over two months. We then came together for a joint consultation with both directors, to review and work further at what was emerging, in relation to the directors' picture, both of the community and its structures and of their own role(s) and relations, including with each other.

A theme that had emerged from the individual consultations, though it took on a different colouring with each director, was that of "letting go". (It is important to note that this phrase was first introduced by the directors themselves, not by the consultants.) "Letting go" sometimes referred to an actual experience or feeling in the director himself that might be tinged with anxiety, and sometimes to what was felt to be a need or requirement of what the directors and senior management generally were seeking to bring about—namely, devolving more authority downwards.

For one director, "letting go" also had another connotation, relating to his impending retirement. (The implications of this, and in particular whether the concept of a dual directorship was necessarily appropriate to leadership of the community, was one element in the initial consultancy brief the directors and council had drawn up.)

It soon became clear, however, that "letting go" and the cluster of emotional experiences associated with it were more pervasive features in the community's life and work. For example, one dilemma in the community was this: A few years earlier a decision had been taken to set up in the main block a separate unit for adolescents. Children from other houses would transfer to this new unit when they reached the age of 14 or 15. From the start the unit had been dogged by many difficulties—for example, around staffing and the behaviour of the children. Staff in other houses were reluctant to let "their" children go and enter this "difficult" new unit. Staff of the new unit in turn complained that only the more "difficult" children were being allowed to enter—that is, they were being used as a dumping ground. Later, another unit had been set up, intended for a few older adolescents, which was to be run as an experimental venture in "semi-independent" living: a kind of preparation for and rehearsal of leaving the community for the world outside. In spite of the fact that this unit was purpose-built and attractively laid out, it had never so far been used.

It seemed that "letting go", and the conflictual, ambivalent feelings surrounding it, were functioning as a "ground bass" to the present emotional experience of this community (a ground bass in the musical sense of providing support to a "harmonic superstructure that colours the movement of the parts above it"—*OED*). In this case, one might suggest, what was being played out against this ground bass of letting go was the relation between the community's past traditions, ethos, and identity and its present and future needs. The directors' announcement and awareness in themselves of this theme was thereby a reflection—or, perhaps more substantially, a literal representation—of the "community within".

During the joint consultation with the directors towards the end of the first phase of work, each returned to the experience of "letting go", in the context of reviewing where they now were in their thinking about their own roles. We, and later they, were struck by a new depressive undertow that coloured what they said and felt. This undertow had to do with feelings of "isolation", of "losing touch with the nuances of the social work aspects of the community", and of concern as to whether the founding spirit of the community was still a living presence in the minds and practice of staff.

Associated with these feelings was, as one director put it, a question as to whether the team managers in post had "sufficient awareness (and capacity) to hold the trust . . . I feel we've lost something, something has weakened. . . . I have a sense of separateness and isolation, which is covered up in the language of letting go." He went on to refer to "a gap, a space" between the directors and the day-to-day work of the units. Subsequently, his colleague used the image of the directors as "disconnected dinosaurs". That morning he had seen someone standing in the hall and realized he did not know who she was. In fact, it turned out to be a speech therapist working in the community.

It would have been possible to read this undertow of depression in terms of the directors' own wrestling with experiences of loss and mourning, at what they had had or were having to give up: direct "hands-on" contact with staff and children; the accumulated symbols, traditions, and rituals associated with the past, when the community had seemed more of a single, undivided whole; the closeness of their previous working relationship. Perhaps the impending retirement of one director, and the fact that his colleague was about to enter hospital for quite a serious operation, acted as a catalyst to such shared emotions.

I would not wish to deny this possibility. But to pursue it seemed at the time to risk missing something else. Just as, earlier, the theme of "letting go" appeared to embody a more pervasive experience of the community as a whole, might not these associated feelings of depression also be giving expression to a wider dynamic in the community's life?

A clue, I vaguely sensed, might be in the language of a felt "gap or space".

This language resonated with something I happened to be reading at the time: a recently published book by a psychiatrist and psychoanalyst, Kenneth Wright (1991), which seeks to explore, through a combination of clinical observation and imaginative speculation, the origins and development of symbol formation and the sense of self. (I state this reference not only because it is important to acknowledge the origin of one's own associations, but also because I believe that the role of chance, or dumb luck, in consultancy, as doubtless in clinical work generally, should not be ignored.)

Wright's argument is complex. It turns essentially on relating successive phases of symbol formulation to shifts, first of all in the infant's relation to its first object—the mother: her breasts, face, arms, voice—through the stage of transitional phenomena as explored by Donald Winnicott, then to the impact of the oedipal situation, when the child faces the encounter with a third position: that of father in relation to mother. In this third position, the gap or space between the child and its object is no longer bridgeable in the same immediate way, but only through the symbol, created or erected in the space between, which is also the space of the mind. In recalling this argument, not in any precise way, I was not trying to make a direct link to what was surfacing in the interface with the directors' experience in this consultation. What happened was, rather, that it brought into view a possible chain of connections between this experience and that of the community more generally.

First of all, it suggested or reminded me that a familiar feeling in relating to adolescents as a parent is that quite suddenly one can become aware of a new and different "gap or space" between one's child and oneself, where it is the child that is creating the distance, or needing the distance, and not just the parent. What can sometimes be very disconcerting is that this need for distance may oscillate with a need or demand for closeness. It occurred to me that the directors' reported experience in relation to staff had something of this quality about it. It was as if the directors were functioning as parents of adolescent children, wanting to let go but disconcerted by and distrustful of the staff's own distancing, separation, from them. I remembered that early on in the consultancy it had been mentioned that some two or three years previously, shortly after an assistant director had been appointed with overall responsibility for therapeutic care, she had referred to her impression of staff as "adolescents". In an earlier session with one of the directors, my colleague had also remarked that she felt filled up with an image of adolescent staff. She had tentatively suggested that the difficulty the community was experiencing in working with adolescents was because there was no place for them to *be* adolescents, since this place was usurped by the staff themselves.

That was one possible link. But another was this: Increasingly children entering the community, as noted earlier, come with experiences of major disturbance and/or abuse. For many of these children, the gap or space between themselves and their early caretakers has not evolved out of and within a normal good-enough experience of mothering. That gap or space, one might say, is one of alienation not separation. For these children, the central therapeutic task of the community is initially to create the absent, lost, or never found experience of being held or contained. Over time, one might imagine that it was this task of holding that had driven the community culture. In the past, as this task was achieved, children would begin to move outside, having more contact with their families or attending local schools. Perhaps this outside contact facilitated the achievement of a more soundly based experience of separation.

Now, however, separation or the achievement of separation is a task that can only be achieved in and by the community, through the patterns of relation between staff and children. Moreover, it is a task that has to be carried out in a context where the establishment of a holding relation is itself more difficult and more precarious. Small wonder, then, that so much ambivalence surrounds the experience of letting go, or the encounter with adolescence.

From this point of view, the directors' experience could again be seen and understood as primary data on the "state of the system", which was inside them as they were inside it—or, rather, once named, not just as data, but as "information", in Gregory Bateson's sense: a difference that makes a difference (Bateson, 1970).

I do not know whether the formulation of the emotional experience of this community, "presented" in the experience of the directors, as I have tried to describe it here, is true, half true, or false. Certainly, aspects of it, fed back to the directors, rang true. But the criterion of truth, finally, must lie with whether or not such a formulation, communicated, promotes development. Since I am describing work in progress, this is a judgement that remains in suspense.

I do not believe, however, that in this form of consultancy, the communication of such a formulation is more than the start of a process. Of course, as in psychoanalytic work, there is no such thing as a definitive formulation. All formulations are tentative: working hypotheses to be tested, which will in turn generate or reveal new and different "thoughts that are there". But I mean something more than this, which is to do with the movement from formulation to action.

Specifically, no such formulation or sequence of formulations can tell a client or show a client what to do. At best it can enhance or release the client's creative capacity to think through what to do. That thinking through moves from a concern with the *meaning* of what is to a concern with the *purpose* of what is, from culture to structure, rules to roles, actuality to intentionality. Nothing I have said should be taken to imply that I do not see these things as legitimate work with the client. I do. Indeed, they are often the hardest work, when the tension between wanting to make a difference and recognizing that only the client can make a difference is most acute.

True action, unlike behaviour, requires formulation. But equally, true formulation, unlike speculation, requires action: taking authority for what one knows, knowing that one may be proved wrong. Within organizational analysis, as I conceive it, one is always moving from the one to the other: formulation to action, action to formulation.

The link is the practice.

Note

First published in *Free Associations, 7* (1997, No. 41): 1–14.

CHAPTER FOUR

The analytic object
in organizational work

"The Analytic Object in Organizational Work" started out in a shortened version written to introduce a dialogue during a social dreaming workshop, directed by Gordon Lawrence at the William Alanson White Institute, New York, in 1994. Under the title, "The Unthought Known", it drew on this evocative phrase of Christopher Bollas (Bollas, 1987) to describe the way in which organizational experiences may embody an emotional undertow, intrinsic to the life of the organization but which has eluded formulation. Drawing on one singular example from a consultancy assignment, it sought to show how bringing this undertow into view illuminated and gave new meaning to the dilemmas and challenges of cultural change.

In 1995, shortly after I had returned to the Tavistock, an extended version of the paper, under the present title, was given at the annual symposium of the International Society for the Psychoanalytic Study of Organizations (ISPSO) held in London.

The paper introduces an implied distinction, which was to be important in a good deal of later work, between the primary task and the "primary process" of the organization. It also describes something of both the functioning and the significance of transference and countertransference processes in the consultant–client pair.

This paper arises out of a mental irritation of my own. This irritation is something I have found myself worrying away at for a number of years in the course of trying to practice organizational consultancy, within a framework and a tradition that is conventionally described as "psychoanalytic *and* systemic". It is this copula that is the source of the irritation.

What kind of coupling is envisaged here? Is it simply the coming together of two frames of reference, with their associated disciplines and methods, each of which is then brought separately to bear on the issues and dilemmas presented by organizational clients? Or is it more like Bion's "reversible perspective", in which the same phenomena can be seen now this way, now that, as in the figure/ground illusions I remember being intrigued by as an undergraduate psychology student? Or again, is it, rather, a clumsy, provisional way of pointing to or naming something new, neither "psychoanalytic" nor "systemic", but "psychoanalytic-and-systemic"—an emergent but not yet fully distributed third?

These may sound like the kind of questions and fine distinctions that can "tease us out of thought" into barren and defensive speculation. For my own part, however, they are emotionally grounded: in the experience of trying to make sense of, or of feeling I cannot make sense of, what I am doing with a client, or of what I am achieving, or of what is going on inside me. At its most discomforting, I may sometimes feel like a professional tinker, with an array of pots and pans culled from experience as an analysand, a group relations consultant, an action researcher, a student of open systems thinking—grasping for whatever seems to be handy at the time. To deal with what? Well, with, I suspect, the muddle, confusion, uncertainty in the pair of us—consultant and client—and our desperation to produce something at the end of the day from *this* coupling.

But now, immediately I have written that, I can begin to discern an answer to these questions. Or rather, not so much an answer as a starting point for exploring them. Because if psychoanalytic practice has taught us anything, it has surely taught us that *its* "object" is disclosed in what happens between a pair of people within the space of an analytic session: what passes or passages between them. And more than this: that what passes or passages between them presents itself in the clothing of muddle, confusion, uncertainty, and fear.

So if there is some analogue of the psychoanalytic encounter in our work with organizational clients, surely it is just here that it is to be found: in the experience of working with the client, face to face, be that client an individual, a team, or even in some sense the organization as a whole.

In what follows, I shall briefly describe one such experience from my recent practice as a consultant. I shall then disobey the injunction against generalizing from the particular (psychoanalysis being, in my view, a science of singularities) and offer elements of an answer to the questions I started from, drawing on this one instance. I could, I believe, draw on others, but to do so would only perhaps be to seek a spurious comfort from numbers. I shall, however, raise some considerations bearing on the limits of generalizability in this domain. These limits, in my view, are roughly equivalent to the limits of what is analysable—or, to put this another way, the boundary conditions within which an analytic approach to working with organizations is possible.

The management of vulnerability

For the past three years I have been working with the chief executive of an authority set up by the Government in 1989 to manage high-security psychiatric services in the United Kingdom, which had previously been the responsibility of the Department of Health and local hospital boards. These services provide psychiatric care for men and women convicted by the courts of offences against the person: physical assault, murder, sexual violence, and abuse.

When I started working with the chief executive, two years in from his appointment, I would see him about once a fortnight for two hours in a consulting-room at The Grubb Institute, where I then practised. The reason for his coming was that since taking up the post of chief executive of this new authority, he had sought to introduce and give leadership to a radical programme of organizational change. The objective of this change, which was one of the underlying reasons for establishing the authority in the first place, was to transform an existing culture in two directions: from a culture of confinement and control to one of containment and therapeutic care, and from a culture of dependence on central authority to one of devolved accountability.

Introducing this programme of change was difficult and was meeting resistance. It was also risky and the public (Government, the media, and local communities) were looking over his shoulder. This public is highly ambivalent: scared and fearful of the dangerousness locked up in these institutions, which it wants to keep out of sight and out of mind, but also feeling some sense of guilt and therefore sensitive to any evidence of ill-treatment and abuse. So, on the one hand, if patients escape there is an immediate outcry; also if once-notorious patients are released. If, on the other hand, a patient commits suicide, kills, or is killed inside, there is clamour for a public enquiry. It produces a report, and heads are expected to roll.

The chief executive knew something of the work my colleagues and I do with organizations. He felt this might be of use to him in thinking through his own experiences as chief executive and the dilemmas and challenges he was facing. We agreed a contract of regular individual consultations, and later he invited me to work with the unit managers of each constituent hospital, if they chose to take this up.

In the early sessions with my client, the work focused on two strands. One was to do with looking at the overall strategy of change that the authority was embarking on and analysing the resistances—internal and external, structural and cultural. The other was trying to understand and get some purchase on the "organization-in-the-mind" of my client, by which I mean the emotional reality of the organization, which is registered in him and is informing his relatedness to the organization, consciously and unconsciously.

For example, one aspect of this reality relates to the way time is structured. It is as if two time scales are simultaneously present, held in tension within the institution and its members. On the one hand, there is a "real" time, with its urgencies and demands: on the other, a kind of illusory timelessness in which nothing will or can change—which reflects in some ways the formal decision of the Courts to commit patients for *indefinite* sentences (the time of "Her Majesty's pleasure").

The work went along quite well, but I was left with a persistent sense of missing the heart of the matter. There was a feeling of being in the presence of something "unknown", elusive but near.

Halfway through the initial series of sessions we had contracted, the chief executive wrote and sent me an "Aide-Memoire on Key Issues Identified". I was particularly struck by one item, in which he referred to the "isolation/vulnerability of the Chief Executive, particularly in an organisation which has no counterparts and which is new, with high profile and ambitious aims".

We had touched on this theme already on several occasions. My client had seen it as an occupational hazard related to his particular role. This was exacerbated by the quality of his relations with the chairman of the authority, to whom he was close but whom he was unable to make use of as a "container" for his own anxieties. I was aware of being used myself in this way, as a kind of surrogate for the chairman. (It was through the chairman that I was first introduced to my client.) However, reading this aide-memoire at that moment, I felt that this explanation did not go far enough. The kind of question I found myself asking was "Why does this system *need* its chief executive to be vulnerable, or to experience vulnerability?"

By this time I had begun working with two of the unit managers of the individual hospitals and with a director of nursing services. I started to notice how each of them from time to time communicated similar feelings, and also the number of occasions sessions had to be cancelled or postponed because of illness. If vulnerability was indeed an occupational hazard, it appeared to be no respecter of persons.

More important than this, I also began to get in touch with my own feelings of vulnerability in the presence of my clients. For example, with one manager, who had voluntarily chosen to start sessions, I had, nonetheless, often felt to be on the receiving end of something akin to hostility: a kind of dead-eyed challenge to say anything useful or illuminating that had a quite physical charge. In short, I felt frightened, both punished and tempted to be punitive in turn. With another manager, I experienced being drawn into being mindlessly reassuring in the presence of evidence of impending catastrophe.

These experiences of vulnerability in the presence of my clients had an institutional undertow, in that I became aware both of feeling the vulnerability of my own institution—what would happen if I made a mess of this assignment—and of feeling the vulnerability of my own relatedness to my institution. I believe these experiences, registered in myself, could be understood as correlates of the experience of my clients. More exactly, I would say that I experienced myself temporarily as both *in* and *of* their institution: something akin to a kind of institutional projective identification.

At some stage in this process I decided to look up "vulnerability" in *Webster's Dictionary*. It is defined there as "capable of being wounded; liable to injury or criticism; subject to being affected injuriously or attacked". I then realized something that I might have spotted earlier: to be in such a hospital *at all*—whether as patient or staff—is surely to put oneself or to be put by others in a position that exposes oneself to being vulnerable, to experiencing one's vulnerability, in *just this sense*.

Moreover, the reason that patients, or most patients, are there is precisely that *their* behaviour has in turn exposed or exploited the vulnerability of others. (I recognize, of course, that this may have involved the patients' own feelings of vulnerability, projected into their victims.) Viewed from this perspective, I now sensed, the managers' feelings of being isolated and vulnerable could be understood as a registration in themselves of an emotional experience that was part and parcel of the life of the whole organization, an experience that arose out of and in turn illuminated the very nature of the task on which all the members of the organization were engaged. As such, these feelings were not so much an occupational hazard as the raw material for work—in processing and responding appropriately to what was happening in the interaction between staff and patients, patients and patients, staff and staff, and the organization as a whole and its context.

I could then formulate this into the thought that these hospitals and those who work in them are presented with the emotional task of "managing vulnerability", or, more exactly, of managing the emotional experiences of *being* vulnerable and of *making others* vulnerable to oneself. This task emerged for me as what might be described as the *primary process*[1] of the institution—not its aim, but rather something without which none of its stated aims were likely to be achieved.

Seen in open systems terminology, you could say that "vulnerability" is the critical "throughput" of this system. Correspondingly, managing the experiences of vulnerability is at the heart of the transformation process the institution engages with. The difficulty is that unless this can be clearly formulated, staff at all levels will be drawn into strategies not of managing this process but, rather, of "coping" with it, through mobilizing personal or institutional defence mechanisms, intended, as it were, to keep vulnerability at a distance—just as I myself had been drawn into doing as a consultant.

What my clients had put me in touch with was how, faced with such an emotional task, one is pulled into projection. As managers of these institutions, they are the recipient of these projections. As a consultant working with them, I am the recipient of *their* projections. As institutions more generally, such psychiatric hospitals are the recipients of society's projections—its fear *of* and its fear *for* what is most vulnerable in itself. Hence the ambivalence: the continuous oscillation between demands that the vulnerability locked up in these hospitals is confined and controlled to keep us safe, and guilt at the cost, the risk, to humane care and treatment.

This formulation, arising out of the space between my clients and myself, released and revealed. It set a new agenda because it clarified where the resistance to the present agenda of change lay, for that agenda implied a capacity to make oneself vulnerable and to handle that experience in new and more emotionally taxing ways. Small wonder it encountered defences. The challenge was to contain this vulnerability, not to control it or project it. But to contain it, it had to be acknowledged not as a *hazard* but as an *occasion*: the occasion for real work—the proof of being in touch and the means of keeping in touch.

What was it that had taken place here, between my clients and myself? I referred earlier to a time during work with the chief executive when I had a sensation of being in the presence of something "unknown", something elusive but near. But I would now see it differently: that my clients and, insofar as I was in emotional touch with them, myself were in the presence of something *known* but not formulated: something "unthought", the organization's way of being, there for the finding.

The "unthought known": the phrase is not mine. It is taken from the work of the British psychoanalyst Christopher Bollas (1987), to which I was introduced by a close colleague during the course of the assignment I have described. Bollas's idea originates from the psychoanalytic encounter between analyst and analysand, but like all creative conjunctions (compare it, for example, with Bion's "thoughts in search of a thinker"), it sets up resonances in other spaces, other contexts.

I think that what I am trying to share can be seen as a bringing-into-view at an organizational level of something *known* in the organization, known in the emotional and physical and perhaps imaginal life of the organization, that has eluded formulation: something primary and ordinary that is *lived* but only as a shadow, and that once formulated, once brought towards thought, paradoxically *creates a difference that makes a difference* to how every decision, policy, action is understood. It does not make things any easier; it does not show a client what to do. But it discloses meaning: it introduces the client, as it were, to the organization-in-himself and himself-in-the-organization. And this disclosure sets a new agenda.

It is not my intention to chart in detail the directions subsequently taken in this assignment. Suffice it to say that the dilemmas and challenges from which we started remain as vivid now as then. The difference is simply in the available repertoire of reflected experience that the client can draw on in thinking through these dilemmas and challenges from the perspective of his or her own role—assessing risks, foreshadowing responses, modulating actions, communicating goals, containing anxieties, releasing energies. Work in progress.

The analytic object

From the vantage point afforded by this encounter I can now return to the question that lies behind the title of the paper: what is "the analytic object in organizational work"? What is it one is looking at, or rather, since it is not just a matter of sight, nor of any one common sense or senses, what is it one is apprehending? I think the simplest answer is: *emotional experience.* But this answer immediately needs qualifying. It is so easy in this culture to regard "emotional experience" as an individual property, bounded by one's own physical or psychic skin. But I do not think that this corresponds to the facts of one's experience. Rather, emotional experience seems to me a property of a human context, or, if you prefer, a relational context, which is both internal and external. In the psychoanalytic encounter, for example, as I understand it, the object of attention is not the emotional experience of either the patient or the analyst alone; it is, rather, a property of the analytic couple and their relatedness to the setting in which their encounter takes place. Similarly, in group work, emotional experience is, as it were, spread across the psychic field created by the meeting of one and another, within a defined or assumed setting.[2]

Organizations, I suggest, can be seen as punctuations of interpersonal space, punctuations defined by the boundary conditions of the organization—to adapt a well-known formulation of Eric Miller's, conditions of task, technology, territory, and time—and by a certain history and a certain culture (Miller, 1959). Thus, in working with organizational clients, I think of what I do or try to do as seeking to bring into view the emotional experience present and presented within such a space, as this is disclosed in the resonances set up in the inner world of my client.

It is this resonance that I have come to see as the meaning of the "organization-in-the-mind". Not the client's mental construct of the organization but, rather, the emotional reality of the organization that is registered in him or her, that is infecting him or her, that can be owned or disowned, displaced or projected, denied, scotomized—that can also be known but unthought.

What is revealed, I believe, at the end of this journey—or at least this is for the moment my working hypothesis—is something about *meaning*: the emotional meaning and significance of what an organization does. This is what I referred to earlier as its "primary process". Or, perhaps more exactly, something about the relation between this meaning and the context within which the organization functions.

Experience both of individual analysis and of group relations are, in my opinion, necessary conditions for the consultant embarking on this journey. But this is not because organizational analysis is in some sense a derived or applied discipline. It is simply because these two fields afford and develop a certain mental disposition, to borrow a term from Gordon Lawrence: the disposition of attention to and formulation of emotional experience and the strategies of evasion deployed to ward off the burden of anxiety such experience may provoke.

Organizational analytic work is *sui generis*, because in some sense the object of attention and formulation is itself *sui generis*. So, for example, I have no doubt that in the practice of this work a key instrument one draws on is akin to what psychoanalysts have identified and explored as countertransference. But countertransference, like transference itself, has a distinct flavour in organizational work in that what is evoked in the consultant is some element or elements in his or her own "organization-in-the-mind", as, in the example I have described, I was put in touch with my own feelings of vulnerability vis-à-vis my own institution.

It is as if all the terms and mechanisms we are acquainted with, either from psychoanalysis or from group relations, have to be reconstrued when the focus shifts from individual or group to organization or, by extension, to society. I think we have only begun to scratch the surface of this re-construction, which, of course, is why this field can seem at the same time so familiar and so unknown.

In conclusion, I want to say something about the client's perspective. Clients do not come into organizational consultancy with the intention of exploring "the emotional experience of the organization that is *in* them but not simply *of* them". They come in because there are dilemmas they are facing, or changes they are seeking to introduce, or practical problems they are having to address—the presenting issues of their organizational world. This is always where one starts. It is these issues that drive the agenda. The consultant's stance is not to ignore or neglect these concerns, but to listen to what the client is saying and to his or her own responses to what the client is saying with what my colleague Jon Stokes has referred to as a "third ear" (Stokes, personal communication). The "third ear", I think, is directed to the music of the "organization-in-the-mind", conveyed in everything the client brings, however anecdotal, personal, idiosyncratic, or sideways on this may sound.

Sometimes the "third ear" may hear very little: one remains and works at the surface issues presented. I do not want to suggest that one cannot do useful work at that level. But where one stays at that level, my experience is always of something lost. If I were pushed to say what was lost, I think my response would be "passion": the sense of engaging with something beyond the instrumentalities of change or structure or adaptation, something that grounds and gives life to the enterprise that the organization frames. I believe that the limits of analysability in this work are no more and no less than the client's openness to that passion.

In a market-driven ideology, preoccupied with what is only too aptly called the "*bottom* line", passion can readily be evacuated in favour of a rather spurious notion of consumer sovereignty. At its best, I am tempted to say, analytic work with organizations may restore something of the passion of the enterprise, as psychoanalytic work may restore the passion of a life.

Notes

First published in *Free Associations*, 11 (2004, No. 57): 79–88.

1. The introduction of this term evokes associations with Freud's famous distinction between primary and secondary processes. This is in part deliberate, since my experience suggests that more often than not the emotional undertow elicited by and intrinsic to the work an organization does is either misattributed to particular individuals or role-holders, as in the case I am describing, or is subject to and concealed by unconscious defensive processes operating across the organization.

2. In saying this, I am not primarily thinking about Bion's conceptualization of "basic assumptions". It is important to remember that, for Bion, basic assumptions are elements within a "proto-mental system": not so much emotional experiences as a defence against the emotional resonance set up within a bounded interpersonal space.

CHAPTER FIVE

The recovery of meaning

"The Recovery of Meaning" was written for the 1996 Symposium of ISPSO in New York and was subsequently published in a slightly revised form in Group Relations, Management, and Organization (French & Vince, 1999). The present chapter returns to the earlier version.

Working from two occasions in consultancy, the paper explores how the re-framing of experiences shared within an organizational context may disclose layers of meaning beyond the purely personal in ways that can both generate and recover organizational insight.

It includes an example of the (spontaneous) recall of dream material in a role consultation, where the remembered dream serves as a container for rather than simply of meaning. This was in turn to initiate something of a sea change in my own practice.

I n the advance publicity for this symposium, we are told that it offers an opportunity to explore "the future of organisations and how psychoanalytic theory can help us understand this future."

I should say at the outset that I have two difficulties with this optimistic statement. The first is that I doubt that psychoanalytic *theory* can help us understand organizations at *any* time. (I am not persuaded that it can help us understand *individuals* at any time either.) What I believe *may* help us to understand organizations at *some* time—and certainly in my experience does help us to understand ourselves in the time of our personal lives—is psychoanalytic practice. Without experience of that practice, on either side of the analytic encounter, no amount of acquaintance with theory is likely to prove all that useful.

Psychoanalysis is an applied discipline, in the sense that it is a discipline applied to the phenomenology of the consulting-room. Theory is extrapolation at best, and the conjunction of such theory with the world of organizations is extrapolation once removed.

I have argued elsewhere (see chapters three and four, this volume) that the relevance of psychoanalytic experience and understanding to working with and thinking about organizations lies primarily in its heuristic value: as a method of attention to and interpretation of emotional experience. I have suggested that this methodology can have an analogue in the organizational domain and that the practice of this analogue can yield insights into the dilemmas, challenges, paradoxes, and discontents of organizations that may elude other methods of enquiry.

Perhaps I am making too much of this objection. I raise it mainly as a way of trying to ground what I say, and mainly to and for myself. When I first began thinking about this paper, I was under the sway of a particular psychoanalytic account of the genesis of meaning and its significance in development. I thought it might be possible to deploy this account in thinking through a number of observations from recent consultancy assignments, each of which in different ways seemed to touch on questions of meaning, and the clients' openness to meaning, as a factor in organizational life.

However, this trial venture proved increasingly difficult and irksome. I felt I was compressing phenomena from one domain into a frame of reference derived from another: nothing quite seemed to fit, without distortion. I was trying to exemplify and apply something "known", when what I had to do was venture out from something "unknown" and risk what links I would find. This paper is the outcome: more tentative, provisional, confused than I had hoped; but by the same token, perhaps, more relevant to the content and the process of this symposium.

Which leads me to the second difficulty I have with the organizers' statement of intent. How can "psychoanalytic theory", or psychoanalytic practice, or indeed any other theory or practice, help us to understand something that is not yet *here*. We may believe that the future can be predicted, although the precedents are not particularly encouraging. One available answer is contained in Bion's evocative phrase, "the shadow of the future cast before" (1976b, p. 309). This could be taken to mean that the seeds of the future exist now, as a kind of inner resonance or presaging of things to come, something that can be captured and given provisional expression. An example that comes immediately to mind, in relation to this setting, is Fred Emery and Eric Trist's (1972) formulation of the theory of turbulent environments and its implications for organizational development.

However, I do not think that this interpretation fully catches Bion's meaning and its emotional undertow. It is hard in this context, for example, not to hear echoes of Freud's image, in "Mourning and Melancholia" (1917e), of "the shadow of the object that fell upon the ego" (p. 249), something impending that heralds loss, abandonment, "catastrophic change" (Bion, 1970). On this reading, the shadow that the future casts *darkens* rather than illumines. It heralds the arrival or return of the *not known*: a world without something or with something unprecedented. (For an alternative reading of Bion's meaning, see van Reekum, 2004.)

I want to argue that it is through encouraging our acceptance of and readiness to receive this darkening that this method of working can most help us, if not to *understand* the future, at least to take the measure of the present in a way that prepares or tunes us to *meet* the future, to *make* it, and to *develop* with it—organizationally no less that personally.

Explorations 1

Some years ago I was invited to work as an external consultant to a one-day meeting of staff working in the Counselling Department of a new university. This department was part of the Student Services Division of the university and was responsible for providing a counselling service for students presenting a variety of emotional or welfare worries and concerns.

The meeting had been planned at the end of the academic year and was intended as an opportunity for staff to reflect together on their experiences during the year and their working relations with each other. (One issue they were facing had to do with a difficulty in sharing and handling anger.) The agenda for the meeting was set by the staff themselves, but at the outset and after a preliminary discussion with the head of department, I proposed the following as a way of getting going.

Each member of staff would find a space in the department's offices where they could reflect alone on their experiences as members of the department: the things they were feeling and thinking in themselves, the patterning of their relations with each other and with the students and staff they met, how they responded to the different situations they encountered. As they reflected in this way, I suggested, they might follow the chain of associations they were making and see if some image or series of images came to mind through which they could visually represent their present picture of the department in the context of the university—with themselves in it and *without using words.*

Large sheets of paper were provided with different coloured pens. After they had drawn their picture, staff were invited to come together again and each in turn to present their picture and talk us through it. Other members would share any associations they had to the picture and, if they wished, comment on the impact that the picture and its imagery made on them.

It came to the turn of a very experienced and long-standing member of the department, who worked on a part-time basis, to present his picture. He then said, with a great deal of feeling, that he had been quite unable to find and draw any image. All he had come up with was a list of single words, which he had scrawled across his sheet of paper. A little later he linked his inability to an experience of feeling, as he put it, "de-centred as a person". He said that he associated this with the feeling in himself that he was not acknowledged by the university as a person, but only as a "hired hand". This in turn, he thought, reflected a number of recent changes and negotiations in respect of his contract.

Things might have been left there—that is, the "no-picture" might have been seen simply as a reflection of one individual's personal and emotional relation to the department and/or the university. However, I found myself increasingly preoccupied along another direction. Might the experience this counsellor had come in touch with in himself also be conveying or mirroring something of the experience of the students he worked with (a reflection of his countertransference)?

At the time this was no more than a vague speculation, which reflected something of my own sense of disorientation in the face of his list of words. But subsequently, as we worked through the pictures and what they might represent, it became possible to see that the feeling of "de-centredness", named in this counsellor's response, had an aptness, an exactness, beyond the emotional boundary of one individual member of staff. What students were presenting in counselling was indeed itself describable, at least in part, through this vivid phrase. They, too, could be said to feel "de-centred" as persons, unable to discover a relation to their institution except as "part-objects": consumers, candidates for examinations, inputs to courses.

I do not want to deny the contribution that the dynamics of late adolescence, for example, or the psychological tensions of transition (from school to college, or home to away) may have made to this feeling. But to emphasize just this aspect of the transference–countertransference relation of students and counsellor risked missing something else, rooted in the organization as a whole and its relatedness to its context. Viewed from an organizational perspective, as a kind of organizational analogue, the counsellor's presented experience registered, contained, and gave expression to a broader institutional dynamic. This dynamic could be seen as one in which, in a rather harsh, competitive climate, the new university's preoccupation with raising student numbers and becoming more "market-oriented" and "cost-effective" was leading implicitly to a construction of students (and by extension of staff) not as *members* of the institution or the college community, relating as whole persons to the whole body of the institution and its corporate life, but more as *contractees*—the means through which the institution made its living, the emotional equivalent of the "hired hand".

What had begun as an expression of one individual's dis-ease with his own relation to the university could now be reframed and given new meaning as a representation within the individual of a more pervasive experience of dis-ease within the whole institution. This "dis-ease" I would see, to use a formulation suggested to me by my colleague at the Tavistock, Jon Stokes, as a factor in the state of mind that *was* the organization, there and then. From this vertex, the counsellor's "no-picture" and its accompanying emotional aura was, one might say, an offering to his colleagues, which through his image of "de-centredness" paradoxically re-centred all their experience.

I believe it is these acts of re-framing that are at the heart of the practice of this mode of consultancy as I understand it. But equally I think they may be at the heart of all creative organizational leadership, which is always moving from "this is what I feel" to "this is the feeling I am aware of in myself"—a move that, as it were, creates a space in which the location of the feeling and its possible organizational meaning can be opened up for *exploration*.

I want to use this experience as a kind of extended definitory hypothesis of what I have in mind by the "*recovery of meaning*". It might be objected that what it illustrates is not so much the *recov*ery of meaning as its *dis*covery. But this would be to miss one element of the experience that I have perhaps elided. When I first began toying with the idea of this paper, I happened to be given a fine account presented by David Taylor, the Chairman of the Adult Department of the Tavistock Clinic, on "some of Bion's ideas on meaning and understanding". At the start of this account, Taylor distinguishes "two approximate general senses" which he intends by the term meaning: "the first is that of general significance—how much or how little, someone or something means to us. An example of this would be the phrase, 'life has a great deal of meaning'. The second is the way in which systems of representation, be it language or pictures, operate as vehicles of human experience" (Taylor, 1997).

I think that these two senses are, in emotional life, intimately linked, in that it is the ability to find or make meaning, in Taylor's second sense, that enables us to recover or restore meaning in his first sense. To return to my illustration, the finding of meaning, and *organizational* meaning beyond the purely personal, in the counsellor's struggle with "systems of representation", seemed also to restore or recover a sense of the meaning of the enterprise of which he and his colleagues were a part: its significance, vitality, and challenge. It mobilized energy, one might say, the energy to address the difficulties and dilemmas that were part and parcel of being a counsellor in this institution in this context here and now—how, for example, to avoid colluding with the tendency to pathologize the individual student, how to work with staff, from the counsellors' position, at the organizational dynamic identified, and how to take appropriate authority for communicating it.

To *dis*cover meaning is to *re*cover meaning, though whether we are able to stay with that recovery depends on more than the moment of insight itself—on our capacity for leadership, for taking risks, for "thinking under fire", as Bion put it.

Explorations 2

I referred earlier to Freud's image of the "shadow of the object falling on the ego". I want to suggest now that the approach to meaning, in the senses I am trying to use and illustrate, always starts under the presence, the sway, of a shadow: an area of darkness in a client's relation to an organization or an organization's relation to its context—something equivalent to the feelings behind the counsellor's no-picture. It follows, I think, that creative work in and with organizations—whether as consultant or leader (which is not the same thing[1])—turns, sooner or later, on the capacity to entertain such shadows.

For the past four years I have been working with the principal of a large college of further education in a deprived, disadvantaged inner-city area[2]. At the time I first started working with her, she had just taken over as principal and was preoccupied with needing, as she saw it, to breathe new life into an institution that in some respects appeared rather closed, embattled, and undermanaged. At the coal face, in the interactions between students and staff, there was exciting work being done, as good as anything she had seen elsewhere. But these interactions appeared privatized, uncoordinated, fragmented, and fragmentary learning encounters. Staff and students inhabited, as it were, a series of dislocated boxes. There was little sense of corporate accountability, lax financial management, and a certain lack of direction. At the same time, within a year, the college would have to face the challenge of incorporation and stand or fall on its own, in a much leaner environment.

For the first two years I worked with her, the main themes of the consultancy concerned her thoughts and plans for renewal. A highly imaginative and powerful woman, she quickly moved to recruit a new governing body and to establish a network of political links with actual and potential stakeholders and other strategic allies from the local community, which was itself committed to "regeneration". Simultaneously, she began to evolve a very original approach to setting in place a new organizational structure, while constantly maintaining a visible presence throughout the college as a strong and inspirational leader.

New staff were recruited into senior positions, new posts created, new curriculum initiatives mounted. Within two years, the college was looking physically and metaphorically quite different. There was a new mission statement, a sharper curriculum focus, new student and staff charters, and a clear sense of direction and purpose.

Half way through the third year I became aware, as did she, of a sea change in her feelings. She was wondering about the future and being tempted with new opportunities elsewhere. Sometimes she appeared almost depressed and preoccupied with the tension and differences she was feeling between those who still represented the old guard and the newcomers. Yet all the evidence was that the place was flourishing. Opportunities for new building were in the offing, exam results were encouraging, and the college was establishing something of a reputation locally and nationally.

I felt, a little dimly, that she was wrestling with things to do with her own relatedness to the college and vice versa. The sea change in her was perhaps a reflection of, and also a response to, the sea change in the college. There was also a parallel between this dynamic and the dynamic around her relation to her own daughter, who was on the threshold of puberty—a parallel she would sometimes bring into sessions as a kind of commentary or counterpart to her organizational experience.

Approaching her fourth year, towards the end of one meeting she suddenly recalled a striking dream from some years back before she took up this post. In the dream *she had taken a baby, wrapped in a blanket, from a brick in a wall which she had removed. She had to fly with the baby in a plane to Israel. All through the flight it remained in the blanket. But when she had landed and unwrapped the blanket, the baby wasn't there: it had "evaporated".*

In recounting the dream in this session, my client was not, I would emphasize, presenting it in a therapeutic context, as an element in a therapeutic exchange or dialogue between us. It was neither relevant nor appropriate, as I saw it, to probe into its possible intrapsychic meaning for her. She was, I assumed, reminded of the dream and offering it for work now, as perhaps having something to say about the situation she was in and which we were trying to understand.

From this perspective, the dream appeared to me to have an immediate transparency as a realization of her current experience and dilemma as principal. The blanketed baby, taken from a brick she had dislodged from the wall, could stand for the baby she had given to the college from the gap in the wall opened by her appointment as principal. (It is relevant to note here that in the early days of the consultancy, she had referred to the college as a fortified castle, inhabited by robber barons.) Israel was the land of promise the baby would inherit.

What, then, of the "evaporated" baby? I felt that this image gave expression to a reality she sensed: that the baby she had both found and made (to borrow Winnicott's phrase), the image of the college she had formed and given life to, was no longer *hers*, to be shaped or moulded or cared for by her. It had, in a graphic phrase she used, "disappeared into the ether".

This linked to, and in turn helped to shape, a transformation in how she conceived of the task she and her senior colleagues were now faced with. She framed this as a shift from *in*tention to *at*tention, from care to support, from minding to mindfulness, from formation to "engagement"—a term she herself drew on and offered.

The recalled dream, you could say, was released by her to release her. In so releasing her and drawing on her own formulation, it changed the terms of her engagement with the college as its principal.

I recognize that there is doubtless far more that could be said about this dream, and I am not wanting to claim any priority for the direction I found myself taking in responding to it. But then, I do not see dreams as containers *of* meaning—a puzzle to be solved once and for all—but rather as containers *for* meaning, available narratives through which we negotiate and seek a formulation for the emotional experiences we register. In this sense, a dream can be seen perhaps as a probe into the world, something available across time, like a kind of personally fashioned deep grammar through which an indefinite number of statements can be made (see Armstrong, 1998).

The dream, I want to suggest, emerged from the *shadow* side of my client's feeling, which the method of consultancy had enabled us *both* to contain without pushing for a premature explanation or resolution. Within that space, she herself, I suggest, discovered its resolution from the repertoire of her inner world. The dream material gave expression to the shadow, the sense of loss, but at the same time pointed to its mutation and, in so pointing, restored the "vital" capacity both to think and to act anew.

Speculations

I referred above to the possibility of seeing dreams and dreaming as "probes into the world", rehearsals or precursors of meaning. Now I find myself wanting to say that the two experiences I have shared carry something of the same significance for me, as if they were a consultant's dreams, through which one probes the world of one's own collaborative interaction with one's clients.

To put this another way, these experiences have been important for me not so much in exemplifying something I already knew, to be deployed as illustrations or realizations of a familiar concept or line of thinking, but rather as generators of something till now unknown—or if known unthought (Bollas, 1987), or if thought not fully acknowledged.

When I first began thinking about this paper, I recalled from many years back an observation of Charles Rycroft's that psychoanalysis was concerned not with causes but with meanings. But it had not occurred to me that one might perhaps claim the same for a psychoanalytically informed approach to consultancy. And indeed, one can look through the literature of this field without coming across much, if any, specific reference to psychoanalytic accounts of the genesis and significance of meaning in human development. Meaning as a dimension of, or rather as a means of processing, taking the measure of, all our experience, that gives life to our relatedness to the worlds we inhabit, that is simultaneously feared, resisted, defended against wherever and whenever it is most needed—meaning in this sense is present in the literature, if at all, implicitly not explicitly.

Alternatively, meaning is relegated to the sphere of each individual's personal inner world, as something that lies beyond the domain of what is specifically public, organizational, or societal. On this view, meaning concerns the nature of the individual's personal relationship to a certain line of work or organization or political standpoint, but not his or her related*ness* to such social objects. I am proposing, on the contrary, that this social world is itself an arena for finding and making meaning and, by the same token, for the avoidance or denial of meaning, in both the linked senses identified in the quotation from David Taylor's paper I cited earlier.

Without reference to this dimension I doubt it is possible fully to understand, for example, the tensions between work-group and basic-assumption mentality (Bion, 1961) or the part played in social affairs by defences against anxiety (Menzies, 1960). For it seems to me that the ground in which such tensions and mechanisms emerge is precisely that in which questions of meaning and our capacity to entertain meaning unconsciously arise: out of the shadow of something felt as lost or unavailable or out of the presence or foreshadowing of something felt as unprecedented or impending (see chapter 10).

It is this last point that I want briefly to touch on further. The two experiences I have shared might be taken from one perspective as instances of the finding or re-finding of meaning, its discovery and recovery in an organizational context. But it is equally important to acknowledge their origin in the experience of the *loss* or *absence* of meaning, with its undertow of feelings of persecution or depression.

To my mind, one of the most signal things we have learnt from psychoanalysis is that what drives development or its counterforce is the way we handle, as infants and as adults, the presence of something absent (but see also the modification of this position offered in chapter nine). For those analysts working under the aegis of Melanie Klein and her successors, meaning is seen as evolving from and within this experience, through the "interaction and emotional exchange with primary objects" (Taylor, 1997). This evolution is, however, never completed, in the sense that experiences of absence or—which I suspect is the same thing, dynamically speaking—of unanticipated presence continually arouse the same primal emotions.

Having said that, I need to acknowledge that, as far as I can at present see, there is no real equivalent in the social sphere of the dynamic interplay between self and object, container and contained, out of which the ability to generate meaning, in good-enough normal circumstances, naturally evolves. And it occurs to me that this may be why, in organizational and social life, *meaning*—that is, the meaning that attaches to organizational and societal experience as a bounded domain—so often, as it were, slips through one's fingers. The result is that the experience of absence or of unanticipated presence, instead of being reflectively held and processed, provokes flight, action/reaction, or withdrawal. (Again, this statement needs to be put alongside the rather different perspective presented in chapter nine.)

I am thinking, for example, of the pervasive use in organizational circles now of the language of "vision", "mission", "core values", and of its accompanying punitive undertow: "downsizing", "de-layering", and "key performance indicators". Too often, such language and concepts seem to short-circuit questions of meaning, as if they are being superimposed from without, rather than generated from within.

I feel something of the same in relation to the current vogue for so-called postmodern theories or accounts, either of the self or of the organization, and their preoccupation with the virtual, the invented identity or the "*management* of meaning". I do not think the virtual is a category in psychic reality, nor that identity is invented, nor that meaning is managed—although, of course, its discovery, as my two earlier experiences suggested, has implications for everything one manages. Such usages and vogues, it seems to me, may operate rather as a kind of manic defence against what is unknown in the face of change, as if the answer to "no x" is "try y".

It is not that some of these things are not important. In much of my own consultancy practice, I work a good deal with organizations on vision, mission, and values in a context of constant change. But I would also feel that such work needs always to be rooted in— or at least to provide space for—the evolution of meaning, which is necessarily provisional and transitional but without which such terms risk a kind of emotional degeneration.

My tentative hypothesis is that what drives such emotional degeneration is the precedence we tend instinctively to give to the claims of survival over those of development. I remember, still with a sense of shock, first coming across one of Bion's more oracular statements:

> I would make a distinction between existence—the capacity to exist—and the ambition or aspiration to have an existence that is worth having—the quality of the existence not the quantity: not the length of one's life, but the quality of that life. There are no scales by which we can weigh quality against quantity, but existence is to be contrasted with the essence of existence. The fact that the patient, like the analyst, [like the world] is still in existence is not adequate. [Bion, 1987a, p. 249]

The contrast between quantity and quality, existence and the essence of existence, is at the heart of the distinction between survival and development that I am trying to draw. What makes it difficult to sustain, in organizational as in personal life, is perhaps this: that when we venture into the territory of the meaning of an experience, we cannot predict what the outcome will be. From this point of view, both experiences I recounted are, as generalizations, over-optimistic. *En route* to the discovery and recovery of meaning, one may confront the unbearable. As with Bion's patient,

> who was quite articulate, in fact articulate enough to make me think that I was analysing him rather well. Indeed the analysis

did go extremely well, but I was beginning to think that nothing was happening. However, the patient checked all that. After a session he went home, sealed up all the crevices throughout his room, turned on the gas, and perished. So there was my highly successful analysis—a very disconcerting result indeed, and no way of finding out or learning for myself what exactly had gone wrong, excepting the fact that it had undoubtedly gone wrong. [Bion, 1987b, p. 246]

There are occasions when there may be very good reasons for feeling persecuted by the unknown. It is just too surprising. At a time when organizations face unique challenges of globalization, radical technological change, and the increasing discrepancy between available resources and the claims we make on those resources, it would take a puritan not to feel some sympathy with the instincts of survival.

Nonetheless, in putting development at risk, through denying or avoiding the need for meaning, the cost of survival will, I suspect, always be the perpetuation of our discontents.

Maybe it is worth it?

Notes

First published in R. French & R. Vince (Eds.), *Group Relations, Management, and Organization* (Oxford: Oxford University Press, 1999), pp. 145–154. Reprinted by permission of Oxford University Press.

1. The difference, in my view, concerns the link between reflective understanding and executive action: while a consultant may need to stay with the client while she or he works through this link, the consultant rarely experiences directly the particular creative challenge involved in the transformation of insight into organizational praxis.

2. Colleges of further education offer a wide variety of mainly vocational courses for school-leavers post-16 years of age and for adults. Since 1993, their governance has passed from local education authorities to self-governing trusts, funded by a national Further Education Funding Council.

CHAPTER SIX

"Psychic retreats": the organizational relevance of a psychoanalytic formulation

"Psychic Retreats" was first presented at the 1998 Symposium of ISPSO, in Jerusalem. The theme of the symposium was: "Drawing Boundaries and Crossing Bridges—Psychoanalytic Perspectives on Alliances, Relationships and Relatedness between Groups, Organizations and Cultures."

The paper was based on a reading of John Steiner's psychoanalytic formulation of "psychic retreats", as these may emerge in clinical work with patients. It traces the ways in which Steiner's concept of the "internal organization" and its genesis can be echoed within experiences of organizational life and the conditions that inform this. A provisional distinction is drawn between the enactment and the in-actment of internal mental states, which I now see as central to the distinction between individual and social "pathology".

In a postscript to the paper, written but not presented at the time, I speculate on the idea of a "psychic retreat in reverse", in which organizational meaning is both denied and evaded through a "privileging of the self".

The language of "pathology" drawn on in this paper needs to be handled with some caution. (See the consideration of this issue in chapter seven.)

The idea of this paper dates back eighteen months, when I first read John Steiner's book, *Psychic Retreats: Pathological Organizations in Psychotic, Neurotic and Borderline Patients* (Steiner, 1993). [Unless otherwise indicated, all citations from Steiner are from his first chapter, "A Theory of Psychic Retreats".]

John Steiner is a Kleinian analyst who works in private practice and was also, until recently, a consultant psychiatrist at the Tavistock Clinic. His book sets out to describe and understand clinical experiences with groups of patients who are "difficult-to-treat" and make "meaningful contact" with. The term "psychic retreat" is introduced to refer to ways in which the patient can withdraw from such contact into states that are "often experienced spatially as if they were places in which the patient could hide" (Steiner, 1993, p. xi).

Such states may appear, consciously or in unconscious phantasy, as literal spaces: a house, cave, fortress, desert. But they may also "take an inter-personal form, usually as an organization of objects or part-objects which offer to provide security [and which] may be represented as a business organization, as a boarding school, as a religious sect, as a totalitarian government or a Mafia-like gang". The patient appears, as it were, to be in liege to this organization, which may be simultaneously feared and idealized.

In his book, Steiner seeks to trace the origin of such states of mind in the patient's attempts to ward off or gain relief from intense anxieties and dread associated with either the paranoid–schizoid or depressive positions, driven by powerful innate destructiveness, or the impact of external trauma, or the intolerance of separation, loss, and an inability to mourn. In more severely disturbed patients, such anxieties may lead to a more or less permanent residence in the retreat, where all contact with the analyst or with external reality appears to be lost. But a retreat may also emerge in the treatment of less disturbed patients, at times when external or internal situations threaten the limits of their capacity to contain mental pain.

Steiner examines and explores with great sensitivity the particular challenges that patients inhabiting or inhabited by such states of mind present to analytic work and the various ways in which one can get drawn into enacting a role within the pathological organization in which the patient is living. For example:

> the analyst may be tolerated only if he submits to the rules imposed by the organization. Pressure is put on him to agree to the limits which the patient sets on what is tolerable and this may mean that certain types of interpretation are either not permitted or not listened to. If the analyst becomes too insistent that his task is to help the patient gain insight and develop, an even more obstinate withdrawal to the retreat may result and an impasse can materialise which is extremely difficult to negotiate. If, on the other hand, the analyst takes too passive a stance, the patient may feel he has given up, and may see the analyst as defeated or dishonestly caught up in a collusion with a perverse organization. [p. 9]

This quotation can serve to illustrate the impact of Steiner's writing on someone coming to his book from a very different experience of emotional work with clients. For it is hard not to read this statement without hearing echoes from one's own struggle, on occasion, to make contact with the world presented—either by individuals or by groups—within organizational consultancy. In fact, I think this metaphor of "echoing" captures a good deal of what passes between psychoanalytic and group or organizational work. But it also has risks. Is it just one's own voice one is hearing back, or is it another's that can help one locate one's own?

I am not qualified to comment in detail on Steiner's clinical argument. My interest is, rather, first, in what that argument suggests about the flow of interaction between, or the interpenetration of, individual and organizational worlds; second, in what the idea of "psychic retreats" may add to our understanding of organizational dynamics in the face of radical environmental or contextual change. Having said that, I need at least to try and capture something of what Steiner means by "pathological organization". For it is this phrase that both gives depth and substance to the concept of the psychic retreat and, in Steiner's usage, evokes the most direct echoes to experiences with groups and organizations.

The "pathological organization" in the inner world

Steiner introduces and deploys this term in two linked senses. On the one hand, it refers to "the organized nature of the process" through which the particular system of defences characteristic of the psychic retreat is constructed. On the other hand, as indicated in the quotation cited earlier, it refers to a concrete and personalized phantasy of an internal organization, made up of objects and part-objects in relation to each other.

In Steiner's account, the origin of these states of mind lies in "the universal problem of dealing with primitive destructiveness", which threatens the integrity of the individual "unless it is adequately contained". Defensive organizations in general "serve to bind, to neutralize and to contain primitive destructiveness whatever its source and are a universal feature of the defensive make-up of all individuals". Where problems relating to such destructiveness are particularly prominent, the defensive organization comes to dominate the psyche. Less disturbing versions, however, can also be identified in neurotic and normal individuals.

Such organizations, Steiner maintains,

> function as a kind of compromise and are as much an expression of the destructiveness as a defence against it. Because of this compromise they are always pathological, even though they may serve an adaptive purpose and provide an area of relief and transient protection. . . . In normal individuals they are brought into play when anxiety exceeds tolerable limits and are relinquished once more when the crisis is over. Nevertheless, they remain potentially available and can serve to take the patient out of contact and give rise to a stuck period of analysis if the analytic work touches on issues at the edge of what is tolerable. [p. 5]

Steiner sees the structure of the defensive organization as linked to the operation of "projective identification". This mechanism of defence was first identified by Melanie Klein (1946) in a famous and hugely influential paper and further elaborated by her colleagues and most notably by Bion (1962). At the simplest level, it refers to the splitting off and projection of a part of the self into an object. "The object relationship which results is then not with a person truly seen as separate, but with the self projected into another person and related to as if it were someone else" (Steiner, 1993, p. 6).

In itself, projective identification is not a pathological mechanism. It forms the basis of "all empathic communication. We project into others to understand better what it feels like to be in their shoes, and an inability or reluctance to do this profoundly affects object relations"(p. 6). This ego-syntonic aspect of projective identification, however, depends on being able to use it "in a flexible and reversible way and thus be able to withdraw projections and to observe and interact with others from a position firmly based in our own identity" (p. 6).

Under internal or external pressure, however,

> such reversibility is obstructed and the patient is unable to regain parts of the self lost through projective identification, and consequently loses touch with aspects of his personality which permanently reside in objects with whom they become identified. Any attribute such as intelligence, warmth, masculinity, aggression, and so on can be projected and disowned in this way and, when reversibility is blocked, results in a depletion of the ego, which no longer has access to the lost parts of the self. At the same time, the object is distorted by having attributed to it the split-off and denied parts of the self. [p. 6]

The outcome can be confusional states where the differentiation between the self and the other is lost or unstable.

Steiner suggests that this can happen when normal processes of splitting break down. In referring to "normal processes of splitting", Steiner is drawing on Klein's view that development in earliest life depends on processes whereby the infant splits its object into good and bad, each associated with different constellations of experience and feeling. This splitting of the object is accompanied by a corresponding split in the ego. A "good" part of the self in relationship with a good object is kept separate in this way from a "bad" part of the self in relation to a bad object. If this split is successfully maintained, good and bad "are kept so separate that no interaction between them takes place" (Steiner, 1993, p. 7). But if it threatens to break down, the individual may try to preserve his equilibrium by turning to the protection of the good object and good parts of the self against the bad object and bad parts of the self. If such measures also fail to maintain an equilibrium, "even more drastic means may be resorted to" (p. 7).

It is important in reading the above to keep in mind, firstly, that what is being described is part of a more extended process—that is, splitting as described here is not the end but the beginning of a story, the prelude to the challenges of the "depressive position", in which split-off parts of the object and the self can be brought together and acknowledged in a more integrated way. Second, one needs to remember that this developmental trajectory is not simply time-related, that it is not ever achieved or passed through once for all. Rather, it recurs wherever and whenever we confront new internal or external disturbances or challenges for which we are mentally unprepared. What is being described is a dynamic that runs throughout our mental life, though, hopefully, earlier experiences, if adequately negotiated, may help us better to sustain the shock of the new.

It is at this point in Steiner's account that the richness and subtlety of his conception of the pathological organization begins to come more clearly into view. In 1957, Bion, in a paper on the differentiation of psychotic and non-psychotic personalities, drew attention to a form of pathological splitting that may occur when, for internal or external reasons, other defences against paranoid–schizoid anxiety break down. In this situation, both object and self, including the individual's mental apparatus, are subjected to fragmentation and forcibly expelled "in a more violent and primitive form of projective identification". To put this another way, it is as if the self and its object are dismantled and spread across the whole psychic field in innumerable bits, each of which contains one not easily identifiable element—a world of what Bion (1957) referred to as "bizarre objects" and later as beta-elements (Bion, 1963).

Pathological organizations may then evolve to collect the fragments, and the result may once again give the impression of a protective good object kept separate from bad ones. Now, however, what appears as a relatively straightforward split between good and bad is in fact the result of a splitting of the personality into several elements, each projected into objects and reassembled in a manner which simulates the containing function of an object. The organization may present itself as a good object protecting the individual from destructive attacks, but in fact its structure is made up of good and bad elements derived from the self and the objects which have been projected into and used as building blocks for the resultant extremely complex organization. [Steiner, 1993, p. 7]

One aspect of this complexity is the ensuing relation between what Steiner refers to as the "dependent self" and this internal organizational structure. For although at times the self may appear as dominated by or as a victim of this organization, he or she is also in identification with and a participant within it.

It is not clear to me how far Steiner's account is bound to the more extreme forms of psychotic processes that Bion and others have described. Certainly, in his book he describes how pathological organizations may surface from time to time in less gravely disturbed patients. For the present, I am inclined to the view, or at least wish to entertain the view, that what he is describing is a process latent and, as it were, realizable in any- and everyone.

To return to Steiner's text, the pathological organization can be seen as the resultant of a process through which "projective identification is not confined to a single object, but, instead, groups of objects are used which are themselves in a relationship". These objects, or part-objects, are constructed out of experiences with people found in the patient's early environment. The resulting fantastic figures of the patient's inner world are sometimes based on actual experiences with bad objects and sometimes represent distortions and misrepresentations of early experience. "What becomes apparent in the here-and-now of the analysis is that these objects, whether they are chosen from those which pre-exist in the environment or created by the individual, are used for specific defensive purposes to bind destructive elements in the personality".

I suggest that this formulation significantly adds to our understanding of what might be termed the social construction of the internal world, although it is not a particularly comforting perspective. I will suggest later that it may equally illuminate aspects of our engagements and enactments in the actual social worlds we live and work in.

But Steiner goes on to make another move, which opens up a more specifically organizational domain. And this is where the second sense of "pathological organization" I referred to earlier comes into its own. Drawing on previous studies by Herbert Rosenfeld (1971) and Donald Meltzer (1968), Steiner describes how the collection or groups of objects into which destructive impulses have been projected

are often assembled into a "gang" which is held together by cruel and violent means. These powerfully structured groups of individuals are represented unconsciously in the patient's inner world [for example, as an internal Mafia] and appear in dreams as an inter-personal version of the retreat. The place of safety is provided by the group who offer protection from both persecution and guilt as long as the patient does not threaten the domination of the gang. The result of these operations is to create a complex network of object relations, each object containing *split-off parts of the self and the group held together in complex ways characteristic of a particular organization.* The organization "contains" the anxiety by offering itself as a protector, and it does so in a perverse way very different from that seen in the case of normal containment. [p. 8; italics added]

The organization becomes "personified": controlling, sanctioning, and protecting as long as it remains unchallenged. Correspondingly, the individual becomes locked into the organization and in a way that makes it difficult to regain, reassemble, and move beyond the fragmentation of the self.

It is not possible to let any single object go, mourn it, and, in the process, withdraw projections from it, because it does not operate in isolation but has powerful links which bind it to other members of the organization. These links are often ruthlessly maintained, with the primary aim of keeping the organization intact. *In fact, the individuals are often experienced as bound inextricably to each other and the containment is felt to be provided by a group of objects treated as if it were a single object; namely, the organization.* [p. 9; italics added]

Steiner argues that where a patient is living in this state of mind, it is not possible or helpful for the analyst "to try to confront or combat the organization head-on. . . . [But] if it can be recognised as one of the facts of life making up the reality of the patient's inner world, then gradually it may become possible to understand it better and as a result to reduce the hold it has on the personality".

Later, Steiner adds that "it is important not only to describe the mental mechanisms which operate at any particular moment but also to discuss their function: that is, not only what is happening but why it is happening—in this instance to try to understand what it is that the patient fears would result if he emerged from the retreat". But he also notes how precarious this move can be:

> Some patients depend on the organization to protect them from primitive states of fragmentation and persecution, and they fear that extreme anxiety would overwhelm them if they were to emerge from the retreat. Others have been able to develop a greater degree of integration but are unable to face the depressive pain and guilt which arise as contact with internal and external reality increases. In either case, emergence to make contact with the analyst may lead to a rapid withdrawal to the retreat and an attempt to regain the previously held equilibrium". [p. 10]

Shifting focus: from the "personalized" organization to the "organization-in-the-mind"

In Steiner's account, the pathological organization emerges as an unconscious personal construct, evolved to offer illusory containment in the face of intense anxiety or mental pain. Suppose, though, that one shifts the focus, from the emotional world of the individual to those of the group and/or organization understood as a *social* and not simply a personal referent. What is it then that Steiner's work may illuminate and contribute to across this bridge?

First of all, in reading Steiner's book I sometimes experienced an uncanny feeling of listening to myself as a member of or in the presence of a group. I am referring partly to the experience of anonymity or of being unable either to locate oneself or others in a way that confirms integrity; also, to the great difficulty one has at times as a consultant in making contact with "the group", which links in my mind to what Steiner has to say about the position of the analyst facing the patient's group or organization in the mind.

This, of course, is territory that Bion described in *Experiences in Groups* and led him to his formulations of group mentality and the differentiation of work-group and basic-assumption functioning.

But I think Steiner's descriptions of the role that the group plays in the inner world of the individual and what drives this role may add significantly to these formulations. In particular, it suggests that we may need to pay more attention than, in my experience, is customary to the fine grain of basic assumptions as these are mobilized in groups and what is driving them: to seek ways of gaining access to the underlying phantasies and the ways in which roles are distributed and interlocked in the service of non-development. All groups can function, if not exclusively, as "psychic retreats". This is implicit in Steiner's account of groups in the internal world. But one can also see evidence that every external "group" potentially constitutes an arena that our latent groupishness, in Steiner's sense, can "cathect", occupy, as it were, collectively.

You may recall that in the introduction to *Experiences in Groups*, Bion states that his "present work" (by which I take it he is referring to his individual analytic practice), "convinces me of the central importance of the Kleinian theories of projective identification and the interplay between the paranoid–schizoid and depressive positions. . . . Without the aid of these two sets of theories I doubt the possibility of any advance in the study of group phenomena" (Bion, 1961, p. 8). I think Steiner's and other Kleinian contributions take this project some way forward, as indeed did Bion's later work. But they have not, as far as I know, been extensively drawn on even by many group relations practitioners, perhaps because the number of those with direct experience of analytic *and* group work is relatively small. One signal exception to this is the paper, "The Fifth Basic Assumption" (Lawrence, Bain, & Gould, 1996), which I refer to later. It is worth noting, however, that much of the response to this paper has been driven by a rather sterile debate along the lines of "how basic is this basic assumption?", as if somehow Bion's triad were set in tablets of stone.

A second implication of Steiner's thinking for our understanding of group and organizational processes is his characterization of the "personalized" organization in the patient's inner world and the way in which this functions as an illusory container of anxiety, offering protection but at the expense of development and the evolution of meaning. This seems to me a very powerful contribution to our understanding of the "organization-in-the-mind". I think this phrase was first used by Pierre Turquet with reference to experience in the Institutional Event in group relations conferences. I have drawn on it myself, as, in slightly different ways, have colleagues at The Grubb Institute, to refer either to people's conscious or unconscious mental constructs of the external organization they are members of, or to the resonance in individual role-holders—especially those operating on the boundary of the organization as a whole—of emotional currents that are a property of the organization as a whole and may relate either to the emotional demands of its task, or to its structuring, or to its relation to the external context—or to all three.

Steiner's formulation of the "organization", and its formation and function in the internal world, has strong echoes with independently arrived-at formulations of the ways in which real-life organizations can function as defences against anxiety. Consider, for example, Isabel Menzies Lyth's account of work in this tradition, offered in a review of psychoanalytic perspectives on social institutions first published some ten years ago (Menzies Lyth, 1989). She is writing of the ways in which the presenting symptoms in an assignment may appear discrepant with the emotional charge that accompanies them and that has led the organization to seek consultancy in the first place:

> I think what may be happening is something like this. There is within the job situation a focus of deep anxiety and distress. Associated with this there is despair about being able to improve matters. The defensive system collusively set up against these feelings consists, first, in fragmentation of the core problem so that it no longer exists in an integrated and recognizable form consciously and openly among those concerned. Secondly, the fragments are projected on to aspects of the ambience of the job situation which are then consciously and honestly, but mistakenly, experienced as the problem about which something needs to be done, usually by someone else. Responsibility has also been fragmented and often projected into unknown others—"Them", the authorities. . . . Such defensive reactions to institutional problems often mean the institution cannot really learn. The solutions tried before had failed, but they will work this time—as though there is a kind of magic about them. Effective resolution can only come when the institution, with or without the help of a consultant, can address

itself to the heart of the matter and not only to its ambience, and introduce relevant changes there. [p. 30]

All the elements in this account—the presence of a focus of deep anxiety and distress accompanied by feelings (conscious or unconscious) of despair; fragmentation of the problem so that it cannot be reflectively held; projection of these fragments as it were across the psychic field of the organization; personalization in terms of an establishment (the authorities) accompanied by a splitting of aspects of one's mental apparatus (responsibility)—are strikingly congruent with Steiner's description of the patient's internal organization.

At the same time, I think Steiner's work adds something to this picture. For example, his rooting of the internal problem in the issue of dealing with primitive destructiveness draws attention to and helps make sense of the strong undertow of hostility, punitiveness, resentment, and grievance that often accompany defensive states in organizations and may be simultaneously and collusively mobilized in a way that makes it difficult to disentangle victim and oppressor. His concept of the illusory container draws attention to the underlying fear of and attack on meaning and helps to account for the difficulty that consultants can face in working in this field, as Isabel Menzies Lyth was to experience herself in her original nursing study. Indeed, this difficulty is compounded in working with actual organizations, since the defensive system, spread across the whole structure of roles and relations, can be very hard to bring into focus. (In my own view, this is somewhat less true where the immediate client is a senior executive post-holder, or at least where one has access to such a post-holder, although I am not sure colleagues in the field would necessarily agree.)

In what follows, I shall use the term "inner-world organization" to refer to Steiner's formulation and "organization-in-the-mind" to refer to what we encounter in real-life organizations.

The consonance between Steiner's inner-world organization and organization-in-the-mind raises some intriguing and ticklish questions. Is what is happening in external organizations an enactment of an internal state, or is it, rather, that external organizations—if I may coin a handy neologism—in-act, or make active, an internal repertoire of response to anxiety? I incline to the latter position, though at the end of the day I am not sure what difference it really makes (cf., however, the firmer statement of this position offered in chapter seven). Another question that arises—and could probably only be answered by practising analysts with experience in both domains—is what happens in a person's internal world if he or she is also a participant in a collusively structured external organization.

Leaving these questions aside, I want to propose the following:

1. Every organization contains a pathological version of itself (a shadow side).

2. This pathological version is collectively and unconsciously constructed in a way that parallels the construction of pathological organizations in the internal world.

3. The function of the pathological version is to serve as a "psychic retreat" when the internal or external situation of the organization threatens the limits of its capacity—as a voluntary assembly cooperating in relation to a "real" task—to contain the psychic challenges of the work. (There is a whole other question of what constitutes "real work" in psychic space, which I think needs addressing. See chapters nine and ten, this volume.)

4. This pathological version is potentially built in to the organization from the outset, not only in relation to what Menzies Lyth refers to as the organization's "ambience", but also including conventional structural arrangements (hierarchies, procedures, and explicit or implicit sets of rules). I am not suggesting that such arrangements are inherently pathological but, rather, that they can readily lend themselves to this purpose. Bion's descriptions of a group's attempt to establish procedures in the early phases of its existence illustrate this neatly (Bion, 1961). More recently Larry Hirschhorn (1997) has persuasively argued that hierarchies may function equally as "illusory containers" (my phrase rather than his).

5. Recourse to or mobilization of the pathological version, as a latent system within the organization, may be temporary or longer-lasting or, at the extreme, chronic. It does not necessarily prevent work from being done, but it interferes with it through

robbing it of vitality and meaning. As a consequence, there is a preoccupation with the political world of the organization: who's in, who's out; the undertow of competitive struggles, gossip, manoeuvring for position, and intrusive personal relations; repetitive and self-sustaining fights over the distribution of resources and/or rewards; or an obsessional search for illusory measurements of performance, which short-circuit the need for human judgement, that is necessarily provisional, qualitative, and subject to error.

6. It is important, nonetheless, not to assume that mobilization of the pathological organization is wholly destructive, although it risks being so. As Steiner illustrates continually in describing his patients, the movement into and out of a psychic retreat may be the only means through which the individual can gradually come to terms with and acknowledge the pain of development. The difficulty is that, as he puts it, "the patient [can] become accustomed and even addicted to the state of affairs in the retreat and gain a kind of perverse gratification from it". This observation, again, seems to me to echo an important aspect of the worlds in which, as organizational consultants, we currently work.

Over the past two or three years, a number of practitioners in the field have challenged or questioned the so-called Tavistock paradigm in organizational consultancy (Palmer, 2000, 2002). I say "so-called", because I do not think there is one such paradigm but, rather, a variety of rather loosely linked conceptual approaches: psychoanalytic, socio-technical, open systems, systemic or psycho-systemic, socio-analytic, and so on. It is suggested that the emphasis on defensive processes and their mode of operation limits the attention paid to the particular challenges that organizations are currently facing, which increasingly concern questions of re-defining the nature and consequently the "requisite structure" of the enterprise (to borrow Elliott Jaques's, 1989, phrase), under conditions of radical technological and environmental change. Larry Hirschhorn's (1999) introduction of the concept of "primary risk", and his recent venture into the worlds of Lacanian analysis and the links between "desire" and mental "flow" (Hirschhorn, 1998), are among a number of examples. And certainly it is true that increasingly we ourselves, in the Tavistock Consultancy Service, are being asked to work with clients on more strategic themes of "re-visioning" the business, or working on "core values", or bringing about "transformational change".

Yet, paradoxically, Steiner's concept of the "psychic retreat" would suggest that it is precisely in such circumstances that the pull towards pathology and the tendency to mobilize latent defen-sive constellations of response are most likely to be in evidence. Moreover, insofar as one consequence of technological and envi-ronmental change has been to challenge our tacit assumptions about boundaries (of task, technology, territory, and time), it is not only our "rational" paradigms of organization that are challenged, but also, as it were, the unconscious investments that those para-digms can elicit: the shadow side of conventional wisdom.

This is well illustrated by Hirschhorn himself in his recent book, *Reworking Authority: Leading and Following in the Post-Modern Or-ganization* (1997). Hirschhorn's central concern is with what might be termed the "psychic costs" of the evolution of what he describes as a "culture of openness", characterized by the apparent suspen-sion or relaxation of organizational boundaries, the attenuation of hierarchy, and the search for more flexible and potentially creative patterns of relationship between role-holders. "The post-modern organization requires that individuals at all levels make them-selves more open to one another—how else can it draw on the individual creativity of all its members?—but faces the stark reality that people don't wish to look incompetent or feel ashamed" (Hirschhorn, 1997, p. 18). Much of the book consists of examples of the various stratagems through which members of the organiza-tion unconsciously seek to ward off these psychic costs of develop-ment.

One such stratagem, for example, familiar enough in other organizational settings, turns on the ritualization of meetings:

> In the past, management meetings . . . were organized as per-formances. Individuals prepared for a meeting so that it could go off without a hitch, so that no real learning or discovery took place. This paradigm for meetings certainly helped all the members contain their anxiety—there would be no surprises; individuals who had performed badly could read the "signal" of the bosses' displeasure without being shamed in public; and

the leader, fully in control, could protect his self-image as highly competent, if not invulnerable. The downside of this paradigm is that managers could not meet to do creative work together. Feeling suppressed by the format but also understanding the larger risks the organization faced, people rushed out of the meeting at breaks to gossip about who was on top and on bottom today, who was scoring points, and who was losing credibility. The gossip relieved their anxiety and returned to them a sense of participating, at least in the "dirt" of the organization, at the cost of failing to contribute to substantive discussions and decisions. [Hirschhorn, 1997, p. 18]

I would see this example as an instance of the mobilization of an available form of "psychic retreat" built in to the unconscious structuring of the organization. The retreat offers "containment", but in an illusory form that forecloses rather than releases development.

Later in the book, Hirschhorn suggests how the "modern organization", when "it functioned well", could contain potentially destabilizing feelings (aroused by real or phantasied dependence) by *depersonalizing* them. Individuals experienced dominance and submission as artefacts of their role relationships. They might, consequently, take a "political" view of their situation—for example, that they were participating in the drama of "labour versus capital"—or they might develop a moral or normative stance—for example, "one should obey one's superiors".

> Similarly, factory supervisors who disciplined workers could protect themselves from feelings of guilt and anxiety by ascribing their harshness to the roles they occupied. While never completely resolving the tension between person and role, the modern organization, by favoring the role, created a paradoxically helpful climate of depersonalization. [p. 33]

Elsewhere, Hirschhorn describes what can happen to such unconscious stratagems where and when, for whatever reason, the gradient of risk increases beyond the capacity of what a particular management finds tolerable. Instead of relying on the role structure to delegate authority, management comes to

> rely on "technical" fixes and disorganizing politics. They try to use technically developed procedures or rules as substitutes

for roles, and they employ the political principle of checks and balances to orchestrate inter-divisional relationships. Checks and balances replace unity of command, rules replace roles, and politics ultimately drives out teamwork. We create a bureaucracy. This suggests that bureaucracy (particularly in high-risk settings) is usefully interpreted not as a rational form of work organization but as a *regressed form of hierarchy*. [pp. 66–67; italics in original]

To my mind, this is a most persuasive description both of how, under developmental anxiety, what I am terming a "psychic retreat" can be mobilized within the organization, and of how the form of this retreat, as it were, borrows from but simultaneously parodies and perverts the very organizational forms that hitherto have served to sustain "good-enough" work.

Every element of organizational life, I suggest, is subject to this kind of unconscious manoeuvre, or perhaps it would be more accurate to say that this kind of manoeuvre is a latent potential in the repertoire of all organizational behaviour. There is something about the organizational (or indeed the societal) domain that elicits it. I think this "something" links to Steiner's account of the function of the organization in the internal world, which—under the pressure of uncertainty, the not-known—real-life organizations collectively cathect.

This is still, for me, the territory in which psychoanalytically informed consultancy has a distinctive contribution to make. I am not wholly convinced that we have much to offer in contributing *directly* to the creative challenges that organizations are facing. If we did, then surely that would be where we would choose to work. But I think we have a great deal to offer in helping, with patience and with sympathy, organizations that are facing such challenges to avoid the misrepresentations and illusory investments that such challenges inevitably evoke.

Postscript

As a postscript to this paper, I want, tentatively, to describe a rather different version of a "psychic retreat" faced currently by organizations. It is a form of retreat that has some links to the constellation that Gordon Lawrence and his co-authors have identified as basic-assumption Me-ness (baM). This they describe as a "temporary cultural phenomenon, salient at this time in history" (Lawrence, Bain, & Gould, 1996, p. 35).

> In particular we are putting forward the idea that as living in contemporary, turbulent societies becomes more risky so the individual is pressed more and more into his or her own inner reality in order to exclude and deny the perceived disturbing realities that are of the outer environment. The inner world becomes thus a comforting one offering succour. . . . Our working hypothesis is that baM occurs when people— . . . meeting to do something in a group—work on the tacit, unconscious assumption that the group is to be a non-group. Only the people present are there to be related to because their shared construct in the mind of "group" is of an undifferentiated mass. They therefore act as if the group had no existence, because if it did exist it would be the source of persecuting experiences. [pp. 33 & 36]

Later in the paper, the authors suggest that this assumption, although serving a defensive purpose, can have its "temporary uses": "There is a sense in which baM can be viewed as a dependency on oneself and one's own resources in order to have a basis of dependability to participate in and hearken to the realities of the environment" (p. 50). In my view, however, this "sophisticated" use, as with the other basic assumptions, is at best precarious. One can compare this with what Steiner has to say about Donald Winnicott's work on transitional objects and transitional spaces:

> There are many similarities between transitional spaces and psychic retreats but also some central differences. In particular is the value given by Winnicott to the transitional area which he sees as a place of cultural and personal development. In my approach, I emphasize them as areas of retreat from reality where no realistic development can take place. In my view, the retreat often serves as a resting place and provides relief from anxiety and pain but it is only as the patient emerges from the retreat that real progress can occur. [Steiner, 1993, p. 41]

The experience that prompted the line of thought I want to describe happened to occur around the time that I first began reading Steiner's book. It took place in the context of a five-day programme entitled "Understanding and Working with Groups", which was one of a series designed and led by the Tavistock Consultancy Service for a number of years and sponsored by a large multinational IT organization. Members attending these programmes came from the sponsoring company and from a variety of other organizations, including large consultancy firms. What stimulated the establishment of the series was the sponsoring company's felt need to develop a more consultancy-based approach to the development and delivery of IT services to client organizations.

The aim of the programme was twofold: to develop skills of facilitation in working with groups and teams, and to explore the dynamics of groups and teams in an organizational setting. The method of work owed something to Harold Bridger's conception of the "double task" in working conferences (Bridger, 2001). Thus, the core event of the programme was a Study Group that had the task, first, of designing a programme of sessions in which each member would have an opportunity to work as a "facilitator" to the group; second, of taking "time out", usually towards the end of each session, to review and comment on the group "process" as different members were experiencing this. Each group met with a consultant present, whose primary focus was on this second task. In addition to these Study Groups there were Consultancy Syndicates where members gave and received individual consultancy to and from each other, in the presence of observers. There were also, on this occasion, large group meetings which all members and staff attended. These were referred to as Whole System Meetings, with the task of "studying the current dynamics of the whole workshop through an exploration of one's actual experience in the here-and-now". Staff worked in these meetings as consultants to this task, which was seen as opening up a more organizational dimension that might illuminate and suggest links to the external organizational worlds that members brought in with them.

For some time the Tavistock staff working on these programmes had been aware of a number of recurring experiences. These included the tendency of members to invest emotional energy in the study groups, while apparently appearing quite listless, fractious, and sceptical in any larger group setting (plenaries, whole system meetings). More significantly, it had become apparent that much of the learning that members felt and said they derived from the programmes was "personalized". That is, they felt they had learned important things about themselves as persons, rather than, for example, as role-holders, members of groups or organizations, and so on. Over time this had led to a covert "institutionalizing" of an unplanned event towards the end of each cycle of study groups, where members "gave feedback" to each other on how they perceived them. These sessions were often extraordinarily intense, almost cathartic, as if they were the culmination of something that had a flavour of personal exposure, of opening up and inviting feelings of vulnerability in oneself and others. They became part of the "myth" surrounding the programmes, passed on in elusive hints to intending future applicants. Within the staff group involved in the programmes, there was considerable, sometimes conflictual, discussion about this development and its legitimacy.

The occasion that set me puzzling was the penultimate session of a study group I had been working with and that had followed much the same pattern I described above. Members were reviewing what they felt they had each gained from their experience. The youngest member of the group, who held a position of considerable responsibility in his company, began talking about how the course had raised for him the question of what was his "true self". (This was not a term that had been used hitherto, nor was there any evidence of familiarity on the part of any member with its more technical origins and use.) He said that it was as if he were in a room that had a glass floor. Beneath this floor was his true self. He felt that there had been a thick carpet on the floor which prevented him seeing and having access to his true self. During the workshop, he said, this carpet had begun to be partly rolled back. The other members of the group, including myself, seemed intensely moved by this image. It set the tone for everything the others said, which had to do with their experience of coming to acknowledge feelings and emotions they had not hitherto allowed themselves fully to recognize or use in the presence of others. These included positive feelings of warmth, concern, and generosity and negative feelings of anger, hostility, and shame.

But these feelings, made public to each other now, were seen as an essentially private matter, one that had little or nothing to say about members' engagement in the public and organizational worlds in which they lived. There was no sense of members feeling that they could take this discovery back into the working world, but only into the world of more intimate relations, within the family or with partners. It was as if, it seemed to me, nothing was to be allowed to disturb or mitigate the very negative, persecutory construction of the organizational world which had emerged in much of the material elsewhere in the workshop. This was presented as a world driven by a survivalist mentality, a world of political manoeuvring, disregard of the human costs of change, which spoke the language of development but was unable truly to act on it.

It then occurred to me that what one might be experiencing—indeed, participating in—was a kind of splitting of the personal and the organizational, which, however important in recovering a fuller sense of self, itself represented a strategy of survival rather than development: a kind of psychic retreat in reverse—that is, a privileging of the self, which leaves the self-in-the-organization exactly where it is.

In his book, *The Claustrum* (1992), Donald Meltzer, in the course of a rather doleful account of the part played by group mentality in mental life, nonetheless makes the point that we would be deceiving ourselves if we thought it possible to carry on an activity with others without participating in the communal aspect, for "there is always a community. And since there is a community, there are problems of organization and communication where the borderland between friendly and hostile, communication and action, governing and ruling, opposing and sabotaging becomes obscure" (Meltzer, 1992, p. 153). We can perhaps retreat psychically from this borderland, but only at the cost of organizational or communal health.

Note

First published in *Free Associations, 11* (2004, No. 57): 57–78.

CHAPTER SEVEN

Emotions in organizations: disturbance or intelligence?

"Emotions in Organizations" offers an overview of the particular perspective on a psychoanalytic approach to understanding organizational experience represented in the previous chapters. It was first presented at the London Symposium of ISPSO in 2000. A shortened version has been published as a contribution to the Tavistock Consultancy Service's survey of its work over the past ten years, in Working Below the Surface: The Emotional Life of Contemporary Organisations *(Huffington, Armstrong, Halton, Hoyle, & Pooley, 2004).*

The paper conceptualizes the organization as an emotionally eliciting mental object and defines four boundary conditions or dimensions that between them generate and shape the patterning of experience. In the process, it reformulates the idea of "emotional intelligence" as a source of information into the nature and functioning of the organization, seen under these conditions.

> If one has the stomach to add the breakages, upheavals,
> distortions, inversions of all this chambermade music one
> stands, given a grain of goodwill, a fair chance of actually
> seeing the whirling dervish, Tumult, son of Thunder, self
> exiled in upon his ego.
>
> James Joyce, *Finnegan's Wake*[1]

Stating the obvious

Every organization is an emotional place. It is an emotional place because it is a human invention, serving human purposes and dependent on human beings to function. And human beings are emotional animals: subject to anger, fear, surprise, disgust, happiness or joy, ease, and dis-ease.

By the same token, organizations are interpersonal places and so necessarily arouse those more complex emotional constellations that shadow all interpersonal relations: love and hate, envy and gratitude, shame and guilt, contempt and pride—the several notes of Joyce's *"chambermade music"*, a wonderfully apt phrase for the emotional choreography each of us weaves, consciously or unconsciously, from our encounter with another, or with others.

To this interpersonal music, I would add the emotional patterning of what Bion referred to as our inheritance as a group species: the simultaneous mobilization of work-group and basic-assumption mentality: dependence, fight–flight, and pairing. Incidentally, it is worth recalling that Bion did not see group mentality as dependent on experiences in groups. It was wired-in from birth, or indeed from conception, as much a factor in our internal worlds as in our external engagements—something we brought to that engagement rather than something generated from within it, *ab initio*.

These are, to my mind, propositional truisms. With the possible exception of Bion's characterization of group mentality, they state something obvious that one hardly needs to be a psychoanalyst or psychologist to recognize and acknowledge. Emotions are constitutive of organizational life because they are constitutive of all human experience. Indeed, neuroscientists have recently suggested that they may be constitutive of consciousness itself (Damasio, 2000).

What psychoanalysis brings and adds is a many-layered account of the *ways* in which emotions shape our experience, their vagaries and vicissitudes (Joyce's *"breakages, upheavals, distortions, inversions"*), their expression in phantasy, their relatedness to primary objects, their distribution across a psychic field that is both internal and external.

This account is intrinsically developmental, in the sense that it emerges from and is in turn verified within a therapeutic encounter. It follows that, insofar as the account is true, it is true because it promotes development; insofar as it promotes development, it promotes development because it is true. Put less contentiously, one might say that the science and the practice of psychoanalysis both illustrate and depend on an assumed link between emotional understanding and mental growth.

Questioning the obvious

From this perspective, it might seem a short step to offering a largely reductive account of organizations as emotional places. On this account, the play of emotions in organizations is essentially *sui generis*. Organizations are seen as a social arena within which we enact the undertow of our emotional inheritance and its economics, as these have been, and continue to be, shaped by past and present experiences. Within this arena, all the dynamic processes and mechanisms identified from psychoanalytic practice (including here Bion's constructions of group mentality) are in flow. The task of the analytically trained practitioner is to reveal this emotional world, as it emerges consciously and unconsciously in behaviour and phantasy. And what makes this revelation useful is just what makes it useful in ordinary analytic work—revelation and development go hand in hand.

Hence the statement sometimes offered by practitioners within our field that the only real difference between psychoanalytic practice with individuals and in organizations is the boundary within which one is making observations.

I want to characterize this position as one that views emotions in organizations primarily as a source of disturbance, but without assuming that disturbance is necessarily dysfunctional. (Nonetheless, it is usually clients' awareness of something *felt* as dysfunctional that brings them into consultancy).

Much both of the writing and practice of analytically oriented research and of consultancy in the organizational field occupies this position, whether the focus is on individuals, groups, teams, or whole organizations. I am thinking, for example, of the work done on narcissistic leadership, or the role of oedipal configurations, or some of the work on group and team dynamics or on inter- and intra-group relations. Within this body of work, the organization as an independent variable, with its own internal logic—political, economic, socio-technical, but also psychic—can easily get lost. Or to put this the other way round, the emotional world of the organization can appear simply as a function, a kind of artefact, of human relations within it.

To say that the only real difference between psychoanalytic work with individuals and in organizations is the boundary within which one is making observations tends to foster the idea that this shift of boundary is not finally of much significance, as if such a shift were merely quantitative rather than qualitative. In what follows, I want to argue, on the contrary, that this shift is qualitative: that we cannot fully understand the place of emotions in organizations without reference to the boundary conditions that define an organization (a *particular* organization) as a human construct. Making this shift, I suggest, significantly affects not so much how we understand the conscious and unconscious processes underlying emotional life in organizations, as their *meaning*: what they have to say about the organization as a system in context. It is in this sense, it seems to me, that emotion in organizations—including all the strategies of defence, denial, projection, and withdrawal—yield intelligence. And it is because they yield intelligence in this way that they may be worth our and our clients' close attention.[2]

An illustration

Before considering this position further I want to offer some material from a recent consultancy assignment as a partial illustration.

This involves my consulting to a client who heads up a team of IT staff working with a group of traders in a large multinational investment bank. The consultation is part of a wider brief negotiated by an American colleague with the boss of the IT division of which my client and his staff are a part. There is a close working relation between the boss and my colleague, and it is partly as a result of this that my client has sought out consultation. Both his boss and himself believe that he will benefit from the opportunity to think through his role and how he works within it. There is also an implication that he needs to hone his management and leadership skills as a prelude to possible promotion. He is aware of a number of apparent inhibitions in his approach to and exercise of those skills.

We start working together, ostensibly on a two- to three-week basis, meeting for two hours. I experience this work together as a tantalizing combination of hopeful feelings on my part—my client is young, bright, attractive, with a lot of technical flair—and frustration, amounting at times to exasperation. Sessions are cancelled or postponed at the last moment, sometimes without notice. Although my client will readily and apparently sincerely acknowledge much of what I try to put words to, it seems to make little or no difference to what he does and the tangles he gets into. I begin to feel we are going round in circles.

One recurring theme has to do with his relations to his boss. His boss is a powerful and dynamic figure, with a highly successful track record. My client knew him from a previous company he had worked in and where he had built his reputation. The two of them had been quite close, socially as well as professionally, and it was through this prior relation that my client had come into his present firm (just as it was through his relation with his boss that he had come into this consultancy). In a series of four enigmatic pictures that, early in the consultancy, my client had drawn to represent how he experienced and felt about himself in his organization, his boss was the only represented figure he had been able to give a name to, placed on top of a kind of gantry, looking ahead.

This relation between the two of them has remained close. They are often on the mobile phone to each other (including during sessions with me) and regularly meet together when they happen to be in the same place at the same time (they are based in different countries).

I should say that, although I have described their formal relation as that of subordinate and boss, the accounting relationship between them does not neatly fit into the conventional pattern of an organization chart. Indeed, one of the many apparently puzzling features of this organizational system as a whole, which my colleague and myself have been aware of from early on, is the difficulty of being able to gain any clear picture of the accountability relationships in play. The IT division serves traders in different parts of the world and trading in a variety of equities. My client is responsible for serving traders dealing in a particular type of equity in a particular country office, but with an additional and developmental global brief. At the time I began working with him, there was no appointed head of IT in this office, though this was on the cards and my client was potentially a candidate for it. Also, since traders can be fiercely attached to their own, local, view of their information needs and since this attachment is likely to influence the ways in which local IT staff work with traders, any attempt to introduce a more global information system is likely to be an exercise in persuasion and certainly not dictat. In short, accountability relations within the division are fluid, and there is no formal, "special" relation between my client and his boss that would distinguish him from a good many of his peers.

Nonetheless, there *is* a "special relation*ship*" between them. It gradually becomes clearer to me that this relationship has a peculiar quality. On the one hand, it is expressed in a close, intimate, and probably collusive form, in which my client takes the role of confidante, back-stop, gossip, bouncer-off of ideas or of judgements—about the business, about the people, about the politics. This relation is shot through with positive feelings of affection, regard, loyalty, and admiration. Less consciously, there is an undertow of envy, which tends to be projected in the guise of disparagement of other senior personnel in the bank, amounting at times to contempt.

On the other hand, the relation can take a masochistic turn, in which my client is continually letting down his boss, other senior staff, and himself, through neglecting aspects of his immediate operational role or not taking up tasks he has been invited to do—for example, organizing off-sites. It is as if letting people down this way is unconsciously and paradoxically a means of testing or proving their commitment or attachment to him.

This relation is replicated in his transference relation to me, and vice versa, in that I continually have the experience of being pulled into a kind of rescue mentality—that is, being mobilized to do something that will save him from the consequences of his actions and, in so doing, demonstrate, as it were, that I genuinely consider him worth saving.

Things came to a head as a result of two events. I have mentioned that there was no appointed head of the IT office in which my client worked and that he was himself a potential candidate for this post—an expectation that he believed his boss had encouraged. Quite suddenly, an appointment to this position was made, from outside the firm. At first my client appeared curiously unaffected (without affect), neither particularly disappointed nor particularly angry. His relationship with his boss continued much as before, but with one significant twist—that he seemed now to transfer something of his "behind-the-scenes" role to his relationship with the new arrival: showing him the ropes, briefing him about the people and the politics, helping out with recruitment of new staff, and so on, while simultaneously, if gently, complaining at the cost to other aspects of his work. In fact, this latter relationship had a new emotional quality to it, in that the element of disparagement was much closer to the surface.

The second event was the completion of a 360-degree feedback for my client, which he had himself requested, once more perhaps following the example of his boss, who had recently done the same and had found it productive. The results from this exercise underlined the extent to which my client was at risk of compromising his good standing, personally and professionally, with his team, his clients (the traders), and senior management by what were seen as puzzling and frustrating inconsistencies in performance, especially in the more management and leadership components of his role.

Again, my client's initial response seemed emotionally flat. He was grateful for what people had said, pleased by the undertow of personal regard in which he was held, and not apparently taken aback by the criticism. This, he felt, confirmed his own view of his "weaknesses", and indeed it was in fact the case that his own self-appraisals were often sharper than those of others.

I wondered if this would turn out to be just another circle we would go round. It did not, however, prove to be so. I had decided, with the encouragement of my colleague, to propose a more active form of engagement, in which we would meet more regularly, at my client's place of work, weekly where possible and at the end of the working day. Almost immediately I was struck by how much more focused he had become, both in how he presented himself and in the material he offered for work. For the first time, he was able to acknowledge something of his anger and disappointment both at himself and towards his boss, but without sourness. At the same time, he began to give up the "behind-the-scenes" role and re-discover and build on his real skills in offering technical leadership, both directly and indirectly. There continued to be setbacks, but it seemed easier now for him to pull back from both the internal and the external pressures to "help out" or "make good", with their accompanying manic edge.

It occurred to me that what the 360-degree appraisal had done was not so much to tell him something that he didn't know about himself, but, coming on the heels of his failure to be appointed as head of the office, as enabling him to *own* what he already knew. To own what he knew in turn implied relinquishing something else, which had shadowed his self-knowledge in a way that robbed it of its emotional meaning—the illusion of the "special relationship".

It would be possible, I think, to read this whole episode, from a clinical perspective, in terms of the enactment of oedipal phantasies, projected onto the relationship between my client and his boss (simultaneously my client and myself) and within a construction of the organization as a kind of extended family. And certainly there were occasions when, in working with my client, I wondered whether what he might rather have gained from was individual therapy, which at one point he was ready to consider. Although he rarely touched on more personal areas of his life and history, I was aware of aspects of both that could have been seen to be part of a piece with his organizational experience. However, and quite apart from considerations of my own competence and the boundaries of our role relationship (I was not working with him as a therapist), to have taken this route, either then or now, would miss the opportunity afforded by a different and more organizational vertex.

In introducing the theme of my client's relation to his boss, I referred to the fluidity of accountability relations generally within the IT division and, indeed, within the bank as a whole. It was as if the whole organization and its various parts ran on the basis of informal relationships: networks of influence and persuasion that cut across and often seemed to subvert what an outsider would consider to be formal accountability lines. As my colleague put it, "there is often an apparent blurring of boundaries and difficulty in staying within the tasks and boundaries of the formal role".

From this perspective, one might consider the more pathological element in my client's relation with his boss as *elicited* (though not determined) by this structural "weakness" or "flaw", within which an internal patterning of object relations could take root and flourish. This might then roughly correspond to what I take to be Elliott Jaques's later position on the relation of psychoanalytic formulations to organizational functioning—which seems to be that, insofar as they are relevant at all, they are relevant only as a signal of the absence of requisite structure (Jaques, 1995).

But this begs the question of what *is* "requisite structure" or, alternatively, of why an apparently "irrequisite structure" has evolved, as if one gets rid of the notion of individual pathology by substituting that of an organizational pathology defined in accordance with an assumed normative organizational model. In fact, my colleague and myself found ourselves struggling for a considerable time with this issue: were we at risk of interpreting the emotional world of this organization in relation to normative assumptions of our own, thereby missing the particular intelligence this world gave access to?

The answer we gradually came to was affirmative—yes, we were. And in arriving at this answer, new light was thrown on my client's construction of the "special relationship". To summarize, and at the cost of some simplification, our hypothesis went as follows: The fluidity of accountability relations and the substitution of networks of influence and persuasion for formal lines of authority was an expression of at least two organizational realities. One corresponded to the developmental situation of the bank as a whole, which was expanding into new areas of business, buying up or buying in new bodies of expertise, often from diverse business and trading cultures. In this context, there was some sense in keeping boundaries fluid and allowing a certain latitude in how things operated, even at the expense of a good deal of both organizational and psychological mess.

The second and more immediately relevant reality concerned the relationship between the IT division in question and its particular users—the business units and their traders. From a structural point of view, the business units are dependent on IT to operate. Furthermore, and increasingly, IT applications can significantly add to the knowledge base of the business, both regionally and globally. In some respects, IT could be seen as a leader in promoting and developing global operations, against the resistance of traders who, as mentioned earlier, can tend to focus, rather, on what they see as their more immediate local needs. On the other hand, it is the traders who traditionally have called the shots as the producers of revenue. For them, IT is simply a service, and a very expensive one at that. In this structural and cultural context, there is a premium on building and cultivating special relations, through whatever means, as vehicles and levers of influence. At the same time, the pay-off from success in so doing can fall well short of felt considerations of equity. To use a very suggestive image offered by my client's boss in another context, the senior traders are seen as the "sun kings" who get all the glory, in a way that can "brew rebellion underneath", feelings of being demeaned and undervalued.

One might say that this is a system that both puts a premium on special relations and simultaneously exacts a certain psychological cost: the inevitability of having to contend with feelings of envy and shame, which cannot be contained within a well-bounded organizational structure. But none of this is necessarily an indicator of dysfunctionality. It may, rather, be an expression of something that is part and parcel of what I would term the "psychic reality" of the organization.

Viewed in this way, my client's construct of the "special relationship" could be seen as a doubtless defensive distortion of an organizational truth: to be understood not simply or not only as the enactment of an oedipal illusion, but as an idiosyncratic response to the *in*-actment of an organizational dynamic. Moreover, this is not just a theoretical point. It has consequences for both the client and the consultant, focusing attention on new questions—for example, about the nature of management and leadership in such a context, or about handling the tensions between personal and role relationships. It conveys intelligence, not just about oneself but about the nature of the "organizational animal" and its present *modus vivendi*: a starting point for further exploration.

To put this point apparently paradoxically: as he began to give up the phantasy of the special relationship, my client was able to get in touch with and explore the world of *special relations* he was indeed part of and how he could best cultivate and manage those relations, both individually and through the ways in which he supported his staff.

Transposing the argument:
from the individual to the group

I am using this illustration to suggest how an emotional constellation presented in the context of organizational work, which may seem to indicate individual pathology, can simultaneously be understood as a signal of and a disguised response to emotional challenges that are part and parcel of effective organizational functioning (given a certain set of conditions).

This argument can readily be transposed from the level of the individual to that of the group. I think that those of us trained in the method of group relations developed by Ken Rice and his colleagues can sometimes fall into the trap of assuming that interpretations of group processes are an *answer* to a question—why do plans go adrift, or decisions get stalled, or conflicts flourish, or feelings of powerlessness, fear, enmity, manic denial, or unrealistic hope proliferate? It seems to me, however, that in organizational contexts, as distinct, say, from group relations conferences, all such interpretations are best seen not so much as answers to such questions but, rather, as re-descriptions of the questions to be asked.

I mentioned earlier that Bion himself thought of group mentality less as a response to what happens in groups than as a core ingredient in all our mental make-up. It follows, I think, that faced with evidence of group mentality in organizational functioning, no less and no more than when we are faced with evidence of individual pathology, we need to ask and be alert to the question: why? Why these experiences in this setting, here and now; what is this possibly saying, revealing about the organization as a whole—its challenges and dilemmas, the nature of what it does, the ways it is structured, its relatedness to its context? In other words, the emotional world of the group, as we become aware of it in organizational life, is itself to be seen as *in*-actment rather than just *en*actment.

What I think can mislead us here is the very model of social systems as a defence against anxiety, which in other respects has contributed so powerfully to understanding the organizational significance of emotional experience. The origins of this model are usually attributed to a paper of Elliott Jaques, first published in 1955, under the title "Social Systems as a Defence against Persecutory and Depressive Anxiety". In this paper, Jaques proposes that, as he was later to put it (Jaques, 1995), individuals unconsciously and collusively "concoct organizations as a means of defence against psychotic anxieties, thereby generating a fundamental cause of problems within those organizations" (1995, p. 343).

On this view, it is as if organizations live two lives: one concerned with consciously addressing the requirements of particular tasks, and one concerned, unconsciously, with "externalizing those impulses and internal objects that would otherwise give rise to psychotic anxiety, and pooling them in the life of the social institutions in which they [as individuals] associate" (Jaques, 1955, p. 479).

One difficulty with this model, and many, though not all, of its later variants, is that it tends to split off the emotional world of the organization from its actual setting in the engagement of individuals with organizational work, within particular structures, and in particular social, economic, and political contexts. (As I will argue later, this is a difficulty that Isabel Menzies Lyth's version of Jaques's model at least in part avoids). Another, related difficulty is that such a model inevitably views emotions in organizations simply as extraneous "noise"—something that needs containing or managing but is not, in itself, a signal of and response to what I will term the reality function of the organization.

Jaques's gradual retraction of his earlier position, over the course of forty years, turns on his bringing into view and formulating a concept of the "organization per se", as "an interconnected system of roles with explicit or implicit mutual accountabilities and authorities":

> All human relationships take place within such role relationships. Some form of organization must be explicitly established, or at least implicitly assumed, before it becomes possible for people to bring themselves or others into relationships with each other by means of taking up roles in the organization. In other words, *organizations have to exist in their own right, before people can collect in them.* [1995, pp. 343–344; italics added]

From this, Jaques now argues that insofar as we are prey to what he terms "psychological stresses" in the work situation, these arise principally out of the "failure to clarify and specify the requirements of roles":

> We get gross mismatches between the difficulty of roles and the capabilities of their incumbents. Or we fail to specify the accountability and authorities in role relationships, and leave it up to the individuals to exercise personal power or otherwise manipulate each other in order somehow to get things done. It all becomes an unpleasant *paranoiagenic zoo.* [1995, p. 344; italics added]

I think there is much to be said for this view. And indeed, the notion of the "paranoiagenic zoo" could itself be taken as an instance of what I have referred to as the ways in which emotional life in organizations can be a signal of, and a response to, some unacknowledged feature of organizational functioning.

However, I do not think that Jaques's structural model of organizations is a rich-enough specification of the organization as an entity "existing in its own right". And, as indicated earlier, I believe Jaques's notion of requisite structure, at least in contemporary environments, begs as many questions as it seems to resolve. Correspondingly, it seems to me, our emotional experience, both positive and negative, in organizations is a richer resource for probing and understanding organizational realities than he allows.

The organization as object

With these considerations in mind, I want now to return to and restate the position from which I started. There is a stronger and a weaker version of this position. I will offer the stronger version, not because it is necessarily more valid but because I find it more heuristically useful in practice. Put simply, the position amounts to the claim that instead of thinking of emotional life *in* organizations (the organization as one of the many arenas in which we live out our emotional inheritance, as individuals or as a species), we should think, rather, of the emotional life *of* organizations (the organization as an eliciting object of emotion).

On this view, every emotional exchange and every patterning of emotional experience within organizations (conscious or unconscious), either in and between individuals or in and between groups, carries some reference to an organizational object. This "object" is an implicit third in all the *"chambermade music"* of organizational life, however intra- and interpersonal, intra- and inter-group that music may appear.

By "organizational object" I mean to refer to something that functions as a point of origin of psychic experience—"in its own right", to borrow Jaques's formulation—but which, like all mental objects, can elicit multiple responses, be subject to multiple readings, more or less conscious and more or less in accordance with reality.

What, then, defines the organization as object? I suggest that it is defined by four boundary conditions (there may be others, but these four are those I am most aware of and alert to in my own work). These are, respectively:

- the organization as contextually embedded (the ecological dimension)
- the organization as enterprise (the identity dimension)
- the organization as process (the task dimension)
- the organization as structure (the management dimension)

It is these four dimensions of the organizational object, I am proposing, that between them generate the emotional patterning within. Conversely the emotional patterning within—whether located in individuals, in groups, or across the whole socio-psychic field—is a carrier, a kind of conduit, of potential intelligence about the organizational object, seen under these four conditions.

The organization as structure and as process

The idea that emotional experience in organizations may reflect and be a function of an organization's structure and process is not new. It has been explicit in much of the work of the Tavistock Institute and Clinic and among colleagues influenced by this work at least since the publication of Isabel Menzies's seminal paper on social systems as a defence against anxiety (Menzies, 1960).

In one respect, the title of Menzies's paper is misleading. It suggests a kind of seamless continuation of Jaques's original thesis—whereas, in fact, I believe it turns this thesis on its head. For Menzies, the origin of the anxiety that mobilizes defences is not in the first place a matter of "concoction". Rather, it is a response to characteristics of the nature of an organization's work—specifically, in her study, the work of nursing. It is this "objective situation", as she calls it, that arouses feelings and associated phantasies linked to "situations that exist in every individual in the deepest and most primitive levels of the mind". Correspondingly, the intensity and complexity of the nurse's anxieties are to be attributed primarily to the "peculiar capacity of the objective features of the work to stimulate afresh these early situations and their accompanying emotion" (Menzies, 1960, pp. 96–97).

It is this "objective" situation, these "objective features" of the work, that trigger the panoply of socially structured defences that Menzies goes on to describe: splitting up the nurse–patient relationship, depersonalization and categorization, detachment and denial of feelings, recourse to rituals of performance, and a variety of methods of diffusing, redistributing, and obscuring the locus of responsibility.

Menzies' work is too well known to this audience to warrant spelling out in detail, even were there time. It is extraordinarily impressive and has remained in many ways unparalleled in the subsequent literature. I want, however, to draw attention to the following:

First of all, I think Menzies underplays, to the point of obscuring, the differences between her position and Jaques's. So she refers to "the need of the members of the organization to use it in the struggle against anxiety . . . to externalize and give substance in objective reality to their characteristic psychic defence mechanisms" (Menzies, 1960, p. 100). For reasons I have already touched on, this seems to me misleading and reductive. It is not that the objective situation somehow meets an internal psychic need; rather, that it elicits an internal psychic constellation and repertoire of response. We are in the territory of *in*-actment and not simply *en*actment.

Second, and here in contradistinction to Jaques's later view, Menzies is able to show how the absence of "requisite structure" is to be seen not so much as a simple failure to understand the structural logic of the organization as object, but as itself predetermined by the defensive mechanisms mobilized in face of the anxieties associated with the work.

Third, and by implication, Menzies' construction of what one might term the psycho-logic of the organization opens up new questions of just what kind of structure in such an organization *would be* requisite—questions that in her original study she was not able fully to explore.

And finally, Menzies offers an account of why such further exploration can be so difficult, since over time the defensive patterning of the organization becomes objectified, as "the way we do things", so that the tension between organizational phantasy and organizational reality is lost. The "organization as object", a subject of inquiry, gets equated with the "organization as given", an object of adaptation. Emotional experience will then be seen not as a source of intelligence, but as a disturbing or frustrating side-effect, to be attributed to individual or group pathology, to the particular characteristics of staff or the vagaries of interpersonal relations.

Much of the later work within the Tavistock tradition has drawn on and made use of Menzies's insights, sometimes coupled with elements derived from group relations theory and/or the open systems framework developed by Eric Trist, Ken Rice, Harold Bridger, and Eric Miller at the Tavistock Institute of Human Relations. Within this tradition, the preoccupation has been with a reading of the emotional life of organizations, conscious and unconscious, in terms of the "goodness of fit" between organizational structures and the psychic demands associated with particular tasks and the processes involved in carrying them out. Simultaneously, the preoccupation has been with charting the various ways in which organizations can get caught in evolving structures and ways of working that are designed to evade the burden of those demands as we register them internally.

Often, however, the relation between emotions aroused by the task and apparently unconnected patterns of behaviour elsewhere in the organization is much closer to the surface. I am thinking, for example, of the way in which the emotions a teacher may struggle to contain in working with children can spill over into her relations to one or other colleague or group of colleagues, gradually becoming fixed in an apparently intractable pattern attributed to personality differences or issues of competence, loyalty, and trust. Such displacements, which often exploit functional or structural boundaries, are, in my experience, ubiquitous in human service institutions and can draw attention not so much to the need for fundamental structural change as for an alertness and ability to process and scan one's experience, as it were, across the organization, to discern its meaning. This process of discernment can, in turn, shed light both on the nature of the work and its psychic demands and on what might be termed the (conscious and unconscious) strategies of containment in play, both individually and organizationally.

Beyond structure and process

It is not only, though, structure and process that define the organization as object. No organization stands alone, insulated from its context, any more than each of us, as individuals, stand alone. While that context is relatively stable or predictable, it may be taken as a given, something an organization needs continually to adapt to, but without having fundamentally to question either what it does or how it does what it does.

I doubt that any of the organizations represented in this room—either those we are members of or those we work with—inhabit such a context. Correspondingly, our experience in and of organizations now is likely to be being shaped as much, if not more, by challenges from without as by anxieties from within. These challenges, I think, as they are registered emotionally, have to do not only with questions of viability—whether or not the organization will survive—but equally with the *cost* of viability—what will and what must be risked in the cause of survival.

Another and perhaps better way of putting this might be that, as the relatedness of the organization to its context becomes more problematic and less predictable, the emotional experience within will both be shaped by and in turn signal questions of identity.

An illustration

Two years ago, I was invited to facilitate an away day for the board members and senior executives of a distinguished mental health trust. The focus of the day was to review and discuss clinical strategy, in the light of major challenges that the organization was facing from outside. These challenges were being driven by political pressures relating to the provision of mental health services, which were in turn related to new arrangements and requirements on the part of commissioners and funders. In response to these challenges, the organization was needing to consider a range of issues concerning the scope and substance of its clinical services and how these could best be presented or marketed to a new configuration of stakeholders, especially purchasers.

Towards the end of the day, I became aware in myself of two pervasive feelings. One was a feeling of an absence—more exactly, the absence of "passion". The other was an accompanying sense of loss, associated with what I knew of the past history of the organization and its founding vision. These feelings were linked in my mind to a difficulty that the meeting appeared to have in formulating a view of what was unique about the organization and its work that could, without embarrassment, inform how it presented itself to the outside world.

I wondered aloud whether these feelings, registered in myself, were being carried by me on behalf of others. I suggested that these missing elements may have tended to restrict the creativity or boldness of people's responses to the various challenges addressed in the review documents. This was not to say that important and constructive work had not been done. But there was something of a flavour of: "None of this is of our choosing, and we wouldn't be embarking on it if we didn't have to."

The response to this observation was muted and hard to read. Was I importing something from outside, linked to my own image of the organization's history and identity, or was I speaking to what was present in the room? I remain unsure. Someone commented that one would not expect passion here. Its locus was, rather, in the day-to-day engagement with patients. But, then, unless one can access such experience in addressing strategic decisions, what guarantees can there be that such decisions may not put the quality and distinctiveness of that engagement at risk?

My sense is that the absence of "passion", understood as the spirit of the work, was serving as a defence against the acknowledgment of risk—or, rather, the acknowledgment of a felt tension between two types of risk: the risk to survival, the viability of the organization in its market; and the risk to identity, the preservation and integrity of a particular enterprise.

Enterprise and context

By "enterprise", I mean to refer to a distinctive practice or set of practices that embody an organization's implicit or explicit concept of the work it does—that define what the social philosopher, Alasdair MacIntyre, has termed its "form of activity"; its conception of the ends and goods involved; its standards of excellence and sources of knowledge (MacIntyre, 1985; see also chapter nine).

The enterprise and the organization are not one and the same. One might think of the relation between them in terms of Bion's model of container and contained.[3] (I do not necessarily assume that the term "enterprise" has a realization in every organization, though I am inclined to think that where this is the case, the organization-as-object will no longer carry meaning, will be experienced as empty.)

Rather than using this model, however, I prefer to view the enterprise as a factor in the "organization-as-object". I suggest that this factor is always potentially held in tension with the outward-facing function of the organization—its contextual embeddedness—just as, in my view, structure is always held in tension with process. This tension surfaces whenever the context in which the organization operates challenges the terms on which and the means through which the organization has, as it were, been trading.

Most, if not all, organizations, be they public or private, are now having to face these challenges. Correspondingly, they experience, consciously or unconsciously, the dilemmas of balancing the claims of survival and growth against the cost to identity, to embodied practice. It is such dilemmas, arising from a dissonance between these two boundary conditions of the organization as object, that underlie much of the emotional experience presented by the clients with whom my colleagues and myself are currently working—be they from banks, consultancy firms, pharmaceutical companies, or schools, colleges, hospitals, or prisons. The forms this experience can take are many and may present themselves as "suitable cases for treatment", either of the individual or of the group: stress, burnout, resistance to change, inter- or intra-group conflict, loss of competence, intractable splitting between managerial and professional functions, and so forth.

I think we are only just beginning to understand the underlying dynamics that relate specifically to this dimension of organizational life and what it may evoke from our inner worlds or our group inheritance. But I remain convinced that we will go seriously astray if we collude with the pull into pathologizing.

No emotional experience in organizational life is a suitable case for treatment. Rather, a resource for thinking, for releasing intelligence.

Notes

First published in C. Huffington, D. Armstrong, W. Halton, L. Hoyle, & J. Pooley (Eds.), *Working Below the Surface: The Emotional Life of Contemporary Organisations* (London: Karnac, 2004), pp. 11–27.
I wish to acknowledge the contribution of past and present colleague at the Tavistock Consultancy Service in formulating the view proposed in this paper of emotions as a source of organizational intelligence. I also owe a particular debt of gratitude to Dr Sharon Horowitz, without whose working collaboration parts of the paper could not have been written.

1. Cited in Ellman (1982), p. 98.

2. Recently, following the publication of a best-selling book by Daniel Goleman, "emotional intelligence" has become something of a mantra in management development circles. Goleman defines "emotional intelligence" as "the capacity for recognising our own feeling and those of others, for motivating ourselves, and for managing emotions well in ourselves and in our relationships" (Goleman, 1998, p. 317). It is not, however, this capacity that I have in mind in referring to "emotions as intelligence". Rather, I am using "intelligence" in the sense of information—a difference that makes a difference—as in, say, "military intelligence". In my view, Goleman's work, however important in its own right, fails to do justice to the potential role of emotional experience as signifier.

3. Bion's later reflections on the various transformations that the relation between container and contained can undergo offer many highly suggestive insights into experiences within an organizational domain, even where this is not his immediate focus (see Bion, 1970, especially chap. 12.)

CHAPTER EIGHT

Keeping on moving

*"Keeping on Moving" was written for a commemorative confer-
ence in honour of Robert Gosling, OBE [1920–2000], held at the
Tavistock Clinic in February 2001.*

*The title of the conference, "Group and Institutional Processes at
Work," made reference to Gosling's lifelong interest in and engagement with this field of work. Trained as a psychiatrist and
later as a psychoanalyst, Gosling joined the Tavistock Clinic as a
senior registrar in the 1950s. For several years, he worked as an
assistant to Michael Balint in his pioneering approach to training
for general practitioners. He became a familiar staff member of
the programme of group relations conferences led by Ken Rice
and later Eric Miller at Leicester and elsewhere, without him ever
losing a quiet but sustained independence of mind. From 1968–
1979 he led the Tavistock Clinic, as Chair of its Professional
Committee, during a period of significant expansion, both in the
extent and range of the Clinic's work.*

*In his practice and occasional publications, Gosling drew on,
without drawing attention to, many strands of his experience*

and training: on early personal experiences of prolonged illness and hospitalization, on his own analysis with Wilfred Bion, on the collaboration with Michael Balint and with colleagues at both the Tavistock Clinic and the Tavistock Institute, but also on his direct experience of engagement in many areas of organizational and social life, as participant, consultant, colleague, and leader.

Writing this paper recapitulated for me something of the tenor of "Names, Thoughts, and Lies" (chapter two). In particular, the importance of allowing for surprise, of not resting on the illusions of the "already known".

In preparing this paper, I was asked to focus on Gosling's published contributions to the field of group and institutional processes. I found it impossible to do this without at the same time recalling and trying to convey something of my experience of the person behind the words. This is where I start from.

I first came across Bob Gosling in the early 1960s. I had quite recently arrived at the Tavistock Institute hot foot from the psychology department in Cambridge to start, as I thought, on some kind of a career as a social psychologist. (The very term now seems to date one.) Social psychology had been my passion at Cambridge, I think because it was the one branch of the subject that seemed to have any political relevance. And politics—of the left-wing variety—were my extracurricular passion at the time.

Social psychology—along with psychoanalysis, and most other aspects of the subject that didn't involve rats, monkeys, or pigeons (I exaggerate a little)—was not taught then in the psychology department. You had to mug up on it for yourself. My tutor, a distinguished American physiological psychologist, Larry Weiskrantz, was sympathetic, but not especially encouraging. He had known a guy called Alex Bavelas, who was doing experimental studies with groups in the United States, and suggested I tried to contact him.

I read all I could but was rather put off by the numerology. Nevertheless, I eventually decided to apply for a Fulbourn Scholarship, ostensibly to carry out research into experimental juries. I recall that in my application I apparently spelled "belief" wrong throughout, and one of my referees had to write to the Selection Committee to say that I really was a little more intelligent than this might suggest. Perhaps it was an unconscious expression of my ambivalence. At any rate, on learning I had been successful, I immediately began to have second thoughts. So I approached my professor for advice.

My professor was Oliver Zangwill, also something of a physiological psychologist, but a highly cultured man (the son of a distinguished novelist), who often gave the impression himself of feeling he had got caught in an experimental cul de sac. He was studiedly lukewarm about the jury idea and told me bluntly but kindly that if social psychology was really my passion, there was only one man in one place it was worth speaking to. And that was Eric Trist at the Tavistock Institute of Human Relations.

I went to see Eric Trist in a rather dingy room at the top of the Tavistock Clinic's old building in Beaumont Street. Four months later, I returned to the building as a raw, opinionated graduate, to start an apprenticeship as a junior project officer within the Institute's action research programme on socio-technical systems: specifically, the impact of automation on work structures in manufacturing industry.

It was a fateful step. In those days, the links between the Institute and the Clinic were still intimate, both socially and professionally. As new recruits, we were encouraged to explore as much of what went on in the building as we could steal time for: attending case conferences, observing groups through the one-way screen, going to as many scientific meetings as we could fit in, and, most of all, through hanging around the coffee-room and bar in the basement of Beaumont Street (later Devonshire Street) listening in to the elders' chat.

For an Oxbridge graduate, trained to be sceptical, in love with words and emotionally naïve, it was at the same time exhilarating and unsettling. What was all this stuff about objects and inner worlds and the significance of a child's play with marbles? Did people really believe, could they really make sense of, what an ex-military man, with all manner of initials after his name, but who insistently and irritatingly disclaimed all expertise, had to say about "experiences in groups"?

Three or four years later, I was lucky enough to be given an opportunity to find an answer to the second of these questions for myself. (It took me another three or four years to take up the opportunity to find answers to the first.) In the mid-1960s, Ken Rice mounted a group relations conference at the Tavistock that was spread over four months. We met once a week in the evenings for small groups, lectures, and application seminars. There were also two inter-group events held at weekends. Ken had managed to engineer a coup and persuade Bion back to take one of the small groups.

By this time the Institute, for reasons the younger staff had difficulty following, had split into two groups, labelled respectively, A and B. One (I think, "A") was led by Eric Trist; one (I think, "B") by Ken Rice. I belonged to A. Relations between the two groups were somewhat frowned upon. I approached Eric. Would it be okay if I applied for Ken's conference? Perhaps a little reluctantly he said, "Yes, of course". So a couple of months or so later I sat in a circle with about ten colleagues waiting abortively for "Dr Bion" to start. The unsettling feelings of the early months at Beaumont Street redoubled—but with an unexpected twist. Some of us, without necessarily grasping a very enigmatic text, had read *Experiences in Groups*. We fully expected, if not to hear about, at least to get some glimmer of understanding of group mentality, and in particular the hidden life of basic assumptions (dependence, fight–flight, and pairing).

Bion never gave the slightest indication of having read this book. We were at sea twice over. He had apparently "moved on"! We were left behind, without ever really knowing what was the behind *he* had left but we hadn't.

By the time it came to the first inter-group event, some of us were in a very rebellious mood. Bob Gosling was on the staff for this event. I recall Ken Rice introducing it, surrounded by his colleagues, and inviting us to form groups of our choice and kick off. Staff would be available for consultancy on request, and the task was to explore or study relations between the groups that were formed. Within three minutes, according to Ken, there was no one remaining in the room. We had all fled into separate groups, apparently at random.

I found myself upstairs, on the second floor of the Institute's new building in Devonshire Street, with about eight mates. We immediately agreed we had no intention to ask for consultancy and would manage ourselves. For one and a half days we remained firmly stuck in the room, sending no one out and smugly waiting for others to come to us. For a while this seemed to work, but the visitors tailed off and we were left sadly adrift. Towards the last afternoon we panicked, requested a consultant, and got Bob.

I cannot recall now what in detail he may have said, except that, whatever it was, it seemed to face us with our fear *of* what was outside and our fear *for* what was inside. To move out was to move on. But to move on was to risk dismantling something: the illusion or fantasy that we knew who we were, what we represented, stood for, believed in; the nature and quality of our (inevitably precarious) attachments. Moving on implied a readiness not to know. We were not ready not to know, because we were so uncertain about what it was that we *did* know.

This memory came flooding back to me as I embarked on reading through Bob Gosling's all-too-rare published articles in preparation for this conference, and I turned up a number of letters we had exchanged in the intervening years. There were other memories also: of listening to Bob lecturing, of discussions in which he had taken part, and of being a member of, I think, the first or second "very small study group" to be mounted at a Leicester conference, for which Bob had been the consultant.

I began to see this first memory and its reference to "moving on" as somehow central both to my experience of the man and to my reading of his work (literally and metaphorically).

It is this notion of "moving on", as presented in the person and the work, that I want to try and capture—not just as a personal tribute, but because I think it has an abiding relevance to the state of the field, to the ways in which we experience and think about group and institutional processes and our engagement with them at the present time.

There is a colloquialism we sometimes use, "movers and shakers", implying that the two are one and the same—or at least that they go together as in love & marriage/horse & carriage. I do not think this is exactly the case. Shakers tend to turn the world upside down, including often the world they were previously in themselves. They move from *A* to *B* (or *A* to *Z*) in a disconcerting way, which leaves us wondering and puzzling about how they got there. Bion was surely something of a shaker, which is why he could be so extraordinarily unsettling. Bob Gosling was not a shaker, in this sense. He always worked within a recognizable and in some ways familiar frame of reference—conceptual, methodological, and institutional—although these frames of reference were themselves often the newfound products of shakers: Freud, Klein, Bion, and collectively the group of psychiatrists, psychologists, and social scientists who between them had reinvented the Tavistock Clinic after the Second World War.

But he was certainly a mover—in that he never *rested* in the familiar, was always testing it against his experience, as a clinician, consultant, teacher, leader. And not only questioning what he knew, but encouraging or joining with others to do the same.

Perhaps the clearest example of this refusal to rest content is afforded in a paper (Gosling, 1981) on his experiences with very small groups (VSG), written for a memorial *Festschrift* for Wilfred Bion. (The VSG was a group of five or so members, meeting with a consultant in the context of a residential group relations conference, with the aim of studying their behaviour as it happened, as the formula goes, in the "here-and-now".)

The rationale behind setting up these groups was the realization that many members coming to these conferences spent much of their working lives engaged in groups of five or so people, rather than the groups of ten or so that conventionally define the boundary of small groups in conferences, let alone the large group made up of all the members. It was assumed that in such smaller groupings, a different range or colouring of dynamics might come into view.

The institution of such groups could, of course, itself be seen as an example of moving on. And indeed, Bob's description of his experiences, and his characterization of the psychological field opened up in this setting, broke new ground: in particular, in his drawing attention to the problem of intimacy as "an impending danger that must always be guarded against", a problem that seemed to put limitations on what could take place, draining energy in a way that could lead members to miss what one described as "the power politics of the small group and all the attendant archaic and crazy events".

It is not, however, this aspect of the paper I want to draw attention to. Having sketched some tentative observations from his first two experiences in taking these groups, Bob goes on to describe a third. This is how he puts it.

No sooner had these thoughts of mine got to the stage of being expressed than I was confronted with the experience of yet another VSG to which what I thought I had learned so far seemed to have only the vaguest relevance. This was a VSG experience in 1977 provided for members of a Training Group numbering 13, in conjunction with a Working Conference membership of 45 and a Conference Staff Group of 12. Training Group members had each had experience of being a member of a Working Conference on at least two occasions before. The aim of the Training Group was to provide them with the experience of assuming the role of consultant to groups of Working Conference members later in the conference. In this setting the two VSGs, one of six members and the other of seven members, remained firmly sub-groups of the 14; it was the Training Group as a whole that held the predominant sentience.

There was much nostalgia for the raw experiences of the SGs [Small Groups] of yester-year; there was some pressure to demonstrate expertise in identifying some small group phenomena that had become familiar; notions of "doing things on behalf of the group" were so quickly mobilized and so firmly ensconced in the orthodox jargon of the group that there was little room left for testing things out in the light of members' personal experience. For my part I had, by accepting a staff role in relation to the Training Group, come to put a premium on the fact that I had worked in two VSGs before and so was more "experienced" than most others. I was constantly hoping that some of the psychological models that had seemed to be fruitful in the past would turn out to be so again. It is unclear how much time was wasted by us all trying to recreate circumstances that would have vindicated the idea that we all had "experience." In fact the salient affective issues in the VSG were of a depressive kind, in particular how one is one's own most dangerous saboteur and how one's public stance on the side of learning turns out to be a determination to repeat what one already knows and to learn as little that is new as possible. This experience left me with two vivid realisations:

1. How much the events I was trying to get to grips with were defined, predicated or determined by their social context and therefore how empty of meaning it was to refer to VSGs, SGs or LGs [Large Groups] as if they were reproducible objects or even that there was such an identifiable category as what I have heard referred to as "conference learning." The initials VSG refer to events that have a certain amount in common, such as number of participants and the fact that they take place in a tradition of exploration called the Leicester Conference, but that are profoundly influenced by what is going on round them in time and place. So much is this the case that any generalization about VSGs that can fairly be made is likely to be so modest as to be of very little use or interest.

2. How quickly a formulation, a concept or a theory loses its enabling quality and becomes a barrier to the possibility of making further observations. An experience of a VSG is deepened or led on to a further and new experience only at the moment that a theory about it is being fashioned. The theory may then lie around for a while to be applied occasionally and enjoyed in a way that is neither productive nor harmful. Sooner or later, however, it becomes a barrier to new experiences, a Procrustean bed and a downright blight. Psychoanalytic practice is also replete with this phenomenon. Perhaps the most that can be hoped for is that this cycle of degeneration, if there is one, is accomplished in as short a time as possible. [Gosling, 1981, pp. 643–644]

I do not think these subversive observations have ever been given the full attention they merit. Seldom have the following been more clearly and simply expressed:

- the relativity of psychological events to a social context
- the danger of generalizing across such contexts
- the tendency to reify objects (VSG, SG, LG, but also perhaps psychoanalysis, group relations, open systems)
- the paradox of learning: that the moment of formulation—the emergence of a model or theory—simultaneously deepens experience and becomes a barrier to new experience.

I think that, for Bob Gosling, all experiential learning, whatever its setting—the psychoanalytic encounter, group relations events, Balint groups—came to be felt by him as taking on a necessarily provisional cast, in which every formulation or theory was for the time being or rather for the *present* time, for time now: simultaneously a point of arrival and a point of departure, from which one had to find the courage to move on.

In an earlier paper (also I think sadly neglected), Bob drew on Donald Winnicott's account of transitional phenomena in early childhood to offer a new perspective on the difficulties involved in this movement on. The paper is titled "Another Source of Conservatism in Groups" (Gosling, 1979). Its focus is on what he terms resistance to change in the face of good reason. In it he reviews two familiar sources of such resistance that psychodynamic studies have focused on:

- reluctance to give up established relationships, reviving internal experiences of loss, and, linked to this

- fear of the unknown, experienced as a realm populated by, as he characteristically puts it (avoiding jargon), "all sorts of hobgoblins and foul fiends" (Gosling, 1979, p. 78).

But he then makes an unexpected move. Drawing on Winnicott's descriptions of transitional phenomena in children's play, he suggests that all or at least most groups, be they "families, teams, working gangs, committee meetings, therapy groups, etc.", create or come to inhabit a transitional zone or space in which the boundary between reality and illusion, objective and subjective worlds, is held in abeyance, allowing for paradox, inconsistency, the play of ideas, the emergence of myths at however rudimentary a level. As he puts it, "[I]t is as if a group soon develops, along with its customary ability to recognize some hard facts for what they are, a similar capacity for indulging illusions and living along with inconsistencies and paradoxes to say nothing of downright lies" (p. 81).

It is this feature of group life that partly accounts, he suggests, for the value we can come to place on group membership:

> In "one's group" one is again allowed to be opinionated, inconsistent, inconsequential, and downright nonsensical. Here

some indulgence of illusions is taken for granted and the place lies strewn with paradoxes. Whether or not the group is engaged in an explicitly avowed common task, such a group has high sentience for its members (Miller & Rice, 1967). This being so, it would not be the least surprising if people clung on to groups that they know either as to membership or as to structure or as to both. For only in such a company where "assumptions" are for the time being accepted as "facts" will the individual feel he has some sanction for his "omnipotence" and so be able to gain some faith in what he is dreaming about but has not yet been able to find in the shared world of objective experience. For this chance to be playful with fellow members of a group and for this reminder of how imagination was first led on by a playful mother, group membership may sometimes be stuck to through thick and thin, and all efforts to change its culture resisted to the death. [pp. 81–82]

On this view, the problem of change is that it involves decision, a choice between alternatives: *a* but not *b*; an either/or that dissolves or cannot allow for contradictions. "Action is felt as 'once and for all' and as a death to the as yet unconceived alternative. At this threat conservatism rears its noble or ugly head!" (p. 82.)

I want to suggest this: All real learning takes place within a transitional space. But the moment of learning dissolves that space, through an act of exclusion. The difficulty is that the evolution, in the individual or the group, brought about by this moment and this act, gets re-incorporated in one's repertoire of response: a kind of so-far-and-no-further, which in turn resists the burden of future experience. Learning and resistance to learning are endless. That is our existential dilemma as learning animals. Or, as Bob expressed this elsewhere, "it is as if learning always has to take place at the edge of exasperation."

I think, though, that it is important to make the point that this is not to be regretted. One other characteristic of Bob Gosling, to my mind, was the way in which he seemed, as it were, to sit loose to psychopathology. One might think of this as a kind of charitableness, born of and from his own more personal experiences and awareness. After all, much of what we may deem pathological is but a heightening or distortion of developmental truths about the human condition: a point it seems to me made quite explicit in the work of Melanie Klein.

So, for example, in an unpublished late paper, "The Everyday Work Group" (Gosling, 1994), Bob sought to rescue basic assumptions from the suggestion, sometimes implicit among group relations practitioners, that they are in some way an unfortunate, archaic hangover from our inheritance as a group species. Without basic assumptions, he suggests, we could not negotiate many of the challenges presented by working life. This was not to deny the conflicts there can be between basic-assumption mentality and work-group functioning. Rather, it was to make the point that the focus on this conflictual element might tell us more about the matrix of psychoanalytic ideas and methods from which they sprang, with its emphasis on mobilizing and probing tension and conflict, than about the realities of our reflected experiences of their presence in group life.

So, too, in the paper I have just cited, Bob sees the transitional territory that groups may inhabit as a potential and not just a constraint. So, having characterized the transitional state of mind in groups, he goes on to say this:

> As people who are often called upon to operate in groups, whether committee meetings, clinical teams, seminars, therapy groups, or what have you, I suggest it is of some importance for us to consider what opportunities for playfulness a group offers, what are the limits that are appropriate, and how are the opportunities for imaginative innovation set up. According to the task in hand the constraints on playfulness may be too great or not great enough, the former resulting in a stilted and sterile group that produces only what its leader already has in mind; and the latter, through its disregard of common reality, resulting in an omnipotence that expands beyond the boundary of the task and that provokes various kinds of artistic behaviour. [Gosling, 1979, p. 82]

I have not time to describe the three illustrations he uses to expand on this point. But I think he is here exploring territory that has great relevance to the organizational worlds we are now inhabiting. So, for example, it could, I think, be said across much of the public sector that the externally driven preoccupation with detailed and intrusive target-setting, quality assurance, clinical governance, and risk management is squeezing out not only the space for professional judgement, but also for the exercise of the kind of unfettered, messy, sometimes playful, sometimes conflictual, imaginative interchange underlying all human creativity, either as individuals or as groups.

On the other hand, in the private sector, perhaps, the saga of the e.com companies illustrates what may happen when the absence of constraints is not great enough and omnipotence extends beyond the boundaries of the task. Though even here we should perhaps be chary of dismissing such experiments as simply illusory, rather than, say, the first, faltering ventures of a revolution.

I have tried to describe something of what has emerged for me in preparing for this memorial paper: the spirit of movement, and the reflections born from it that I felt I was picking up in memory and from the words on the page, and their abiding professional challenge to us, certainly to myself.

Before closing, I want to say something that, it has occurred to me, may have helped and served to inform the particular emphases I have picked out from Bob Gosling's work. There may have been more personal elements, also, but they are not available to me. There are two aspects I want to comment on: the range and variability of Bob Gosling's professional activities and interests, and the constancy of a certain mental practice.

Bob trained as a psychiatrist and a psychoanalyst and was a distinguished practitioner in those disciplines. But he did not confine himself to them. The impression I have is that his centre of interest always lay in what one might think of as applied fields, except that the language of application does not do justice exactly to what is involved.

To put this another way—and perhaps this is what Sebastian Kraemer meant when he described Bob Gosling to me a few days ago as a "quintessentially Tavistock man"—Bob was always putting his psychoanalytic knowledge and understanding, including here his knowledge and understanding of group relations, both to the service and to the test of engagement with other areas of experience and practice: work with families, general medical practice, the interaction of students and teachers, the leadership of professional support groups, the management of institutions.

He moved himself between such social contexts, and I think it was this moving *between* that both drew his attention to and enabled him so clearly to formulate, from his own experience, the necessity and the difficulty of moving on.

Nonetheless, in this movement between there was also something held constant that characterized his practice and surely reflected something from his psychoanalytic training and experience. In the chapter he wrote with Pierre Turquet, "The Training of General Practitioners" (Gosling & Turquet, 1967), which describes the approach developed by the two of them to working with Balint groups, they state their objective as follows: "Our problem is so to conduct a seminar that there is little or no denying or evading of the emotional welter in which the GP is living his professional life" (pp. 14–15).

A little later, referring to the role of the group leader, they say: "The leader's aim is to assist the egos of the member to embrace more, to experience more fully the forces current in their relations with their patients" (p. 33).

To combine these two images, I think it is this stance of encouraging us, whatever the context we inhabit, to embrace the emotional welter in which we work and live that perhaps best sums up Bob's enterprise, as it were across the board. Not as something from which he stood apart, but as something he was necessarily also implicated in and attuned to. Necessarily, because it is only through being implicated, through recognizing one's own implicatedness, that one gets access to what is happening.

And this enterprise for Bob was not something engaged in simply for its own sake, but because it made a difference to us, carried information, intelligence, about the worlds of thought and action we inhabit, and the dilemmas and challenges we face.

For myself and my colleagues, it is an exemplary stance and one that I believe, if we can be true to it, helps us, with our clients, to keep on moving on.

Note

First published in *Free Associations*, 10 (2003, No. 53): 1–13.

CHAPTER NINE

Making present: reflections on a neglected function of leadership and its contemporary relevance

"Making Present" was presented in September 2001 at the conference organized by the Organisation for Promoting Understanding of Society (OPUS) to launch the journal Organisational and Social Dynamics.

The stimulus for the paper was a sensed link between recent developments in child psychotherapy, associated with the work of Anne Alvarez at the Tavistock Clinic, and current experiences of working with chief executives and others in leadership positions.

Alvarez's work has drawn attention to the importance in psychic development of the ways in which the interaction of mother and baby establishes a sense of lively presence, "complex, varied and constantly changing . . . pleasurable but in a demanding way". This sense of presence both stimulates development and serves to modify the impact of absence. In these ways, it acts as both an origin and a precursor of thoughts.

The paper explores a number of ways in which the idea of the modulation and regulation of presence challenges and extends

our understanding of leadership, especially in contemporary or-
ganizations. It suggests that part of the function of leadership un-
der conditions of radical uncertainty, contextual and structural,
is to make present, through interaction with others, an idea of
and a feel for the "enterprise"—or "practice"—of the organiza-
tion which can ground and recover the exchange and enact-
ment of thought. It proposes that this function modifies and adds
to the preoccupation with both the directional and the contain-
ing aspects of leadership which have informed much of the dis-
cussion of this topic within the Tavistock tradition.

In writing this paper, I was aware of entering new territory, and
this may account for its somewhat speculative air. At the time, it
was suggested the paper needed filling out to illustrate the argu-
ment, drawing on case examples. The intention, however, was
less to exemplify something as to open up a, hopefully sugges-
tive, line of enquiry. In this version, I have added some riders in
response to particular criticisms from colleagues during discus-
sion but have otherwise chosen to let it stand.

One of the privileges of practising as an organizational
consultant in my own institution is the access one has to
the thinking and perspectives of colleagues from other
psychoanalytically informed disciplines. The ideas about organizational leadership that I want to explore, in a provisional way, owe
their origin to listening to two child psychotherapists, Branca
Pecotic and Anne Alvarez, on different occasions over the past
eighteen months.

Branca Pecotic, apart from her therapeutic practice, has been
interested in exploring the "Tavistock Approach to Groups and
Institutions" and the contribution this can make to the training of
child psychotherapists, many of whom will be working within
organizational settings. In a paper first sketched out to Anton
Obholzer's "Consulting to Institutions" workshop at the Tavistock
Clinic, she offered a number of observations on what she saw as a
tendency within this approach to overemphasize the destructive
and pathological aspects of group and organizational functioning.
This emphasis, she argued, risked obscuring the extent to which,

for example, defensive processes or strategies can simultaneously carry within them, as a shadow, a stimulus for growth and development. As she puts it:

> the defenses are a sign that something is moving on . . . . Whatever the defensive culture in the group or institution is, it may be viewed as a communication of an inner struggle, of a conflict between the need to change, adapt or grow and the difficulty in doing so for fear of disintegration or painful loss of identity. [Pecotic, 2000][1]

This observation links to a further point Pecotic goes on to make: that while

> the Kleinian authors who have written about groups and institutions have tended to emphasize both the defensive nature of institutions as well as their function of containing anxieties and psychic pain, [they have written] little of those aspects of the containing object that promote growth and development.

This contrasts with some recent work in child psychotherapy, which has drawn attention to the capacity of

> the object not only to contain anxieties, to digest primitive communications of dread and pain, but also as being able to receive, augment and return back something that might be described simply as *"joie de vivre"* . . . pleasures of discovery of the world and discoveries within oneself . . . . If that is missing, then the child feels that there is no meeting point between his object and himself in the areas of pleasure, joys of growth etc. Only the pain is understood.

It is this observation that has set me thinking about "a neglected function of leadership". But why, then, "making present?" Around the same time as listening to Branca Pecotic, I attended a Scientific Meeting at the Tavistock at which Anne Alvarez was reading a paper based on her work over many years with autistic and seriously disturbed young children. In this paper, Alvarez referred to various respects in which her experience of working with her young patients had gradually led her to question "the emphasis in some psychoanalytic theories on frustration as the major impetus for learning" (Alvarez, 1999, p. 184).

She cites, for example, Freud's assertion that "it is the experiences of unpleasure that educate us and introduce us to 'reality'", as in infancy and early childhood the baby gradually learns the truth that "he is lord and master of neither his mother, nor the universe" (Alvarez, 1999, p. 184). Later, Wilfred Bion, reframing Freud's observations in the light of Melanie Klein's views, offered a two-stage model of the genesis of learning: "first, that a preconception [something like a primitive expectation of the object] had to meet with a realization for a conception to be born, and, second, that a conception had to meet with a frustration [the absence of the object and/or the satisfaction derived from it] for a thought to be born" (Alvarez, 1999, p. 185). Most of Bion's attention, however, Alvarez suggests, focused on this second step rather than the first.

This second step, though, is consequent on the first, in the same way that absence is consequent on an experience of presence. Alvarez was concerned to show how, for many of her young patients, the deep emotional and cognitive disturbances from which they suffered were linked not so much, or not primarily, to anxieties and anger about *losing* the object as to anxieties and despair about *finding* it. These anxieties and despair might be the consequence of severe early trauma or neglect or of some developmental deficit in the child's earliest interactions with its mother or carer. In either case, it was as if the child had no experience of a constant and stable object on which to draw, to internalize, project into, love, hate, know, miss, and, correspondingly, no continuing sense of its own identity. The dynamics of object relatedness, so important for development, had too little soil to grow on.

Alvarez argues that the establishment of presence is an achievement of normal development in the parent–child dyad, an achievement she describes as "pleasurable, but in a demanding way" (p. 193). This establishment of presence is neither passive, nor static. One might rather say that it is co-created in the interplay between parent and child through which the child begins to get to know, "reflectively and cognitively, as well as emotionally . . . the whatness, the is-ness" of the object (p. 194).

This evocative phrase brought to mind a number of recent experiences in working with clients from different organizational settings, each of whom were facing dilemmas and challenges relating to their exercise of leadership which did not seem to be contained within a familiar conceptual frame. It seemed to offer a new way of understanding what we were exploring.

Drawing on Alvarez's formulation, I want to suggest that it is part of the function of leadership to serve an analogous process of making present in the interplay with others, "reflectively and cognitively, as well as emotionally, the whatness, the is-ness" of the *organizational* object (cf. chapter seven).

I want further to suggest that neglect of this function not only reduces the vitality of people's engagement with organizations, but can lead to misinterpreting the dynamics of apparent defensiveness and resistance to change and what these may be communicating. Correspondingly, such mis-interpretations set limits to real organizational creativity in the face of new environmental challenges or threats.

What, then, might be meant by this somewhat enigmatic phrase, "the whatness, the is-ness of the organizational object"?

It has been characteristic of the "open systems" approach to organizations pioneered by the Tavistock Institute, to emphasize the notion of "primary task", as the defining characteristic of the organization. Thus, in a recent paper, "The Leader, the Unconscious, and the Management of the Organisation", written for a collection of papers in honour of Eric Miller, Anton Obholzer refers to an awareness of the primary task of the organization as "the main institutional 'ballast' that keeps the organization, both membership and leadership, steady" (Obholzer, 2001, p. 198). Correspondingly, in Obholzer's view, one of the core elements of the task of leadership is "to see that the concept of the primary task of the organization is not only uppermost in the minds of all the members of the organization, but that it is constantly reviewed in the light of the external environment and that the functioning, structure, and staffing of the organisation changes in accordance with the changing primary task and its cluster of subtasks" (p. 199).

Since Ken Rice first introduced the term "primary task" in the late 1950s, it has spawned endless discussion and controversy (e.g., Lawrence, 1985; Miller, 1993; Miller & Rice, 1967; Rice, 1958, 1963): Is the term to be defined normatively, existentially, or phenomenologically? Is it always exclusive, or can there be more than one such task? How far does it prioritize questions of survival over questions of development?

I have no doubt that the concept often has considerable heuristic value, serving to sharpen and clarify the relation between organizational processes: of import, conversion, and export. But I do not think it gets close to defining the "whatness, the is-ness" of the organization. Nor do I think one gets much further by grafting on to primary task some notion of organizational culture or sentient systems as partly independent but linked variables, emerging to contain anxieties or satisfy unmet human and social needs.

"Primary task" is fundamentally an instrumental notion tied to a concept of external goals or objectives, either explicit or implicit. Its focus is on the end result, actual or anticipated. What is not captured is the journeying; or, rather, the journeying is simply read back from the end result, as if, for example, the object of a game were only to win.

It may be useful here to draw a distinction between organization and enterprise. I understand that in its original French meaning, "*entreprise*" has the connotation of "an organisation of man [*sic*] and materials around some human endeavour". I suggest that it is this idea of "endeavour" that is the carrier of organizational identity, that defines or signals the organizational object: its "whatness and is-ness".

But this only puts the question one step back. What is the carrier of "endeavour"? What does "endeavour" describe or imply? I want to draw here not from psychoanalysis, but from the work of the social philosopher Alasdair MacIntyre. In a book published some twenty years ago, *After Virtue: A Study in Moral Theory*[2] (1985), and within the context of a critique of managerialism, MacIntyre refers to what he calls a "practice". This is how he defines it:

> any coherent and complex form of socially established cooperative human activity through which goods internal to that form of activity are realized in the course of trying to achieve those standards of excellence which are appropriate to, and partially definitive of, that form of activity, with the result that human powers to achieve excellence, and human conceptions of the ends and goods involved, are systematically extended.
> [MacIntyre, 1985, p. 187]

There are a number of features of this definition I want to draw attention to. First of all, its reference to internally derived criteria— that is, criteria arising from the nature or logic (or psycho-logic) of the activity itself: say, parenting, teaching, playing cricket, or chess (an example MacIntyre himself uses); or again, say, psychoanalysis, preaching, fishing, banking, running a business. Second, its reference to "ends and goods", terms that carry an evaluative connotation that is expressive rather than just instrumental. Third, its developmental emphasis on achieving excellence and the extension of human powers. To these features one might add an implicit undertow of commitment or passion—of doing well.

MacIntyre draws a distinction between internal and external goods, and this distinction is important to later steps in the argument. Internal goods are goods that are intrinsic to a practice; that can only be specified in terms of the practice, through examples rather than abstractions; and that can only be identified and recognized through the experience of participating in the practice in question: "[t]hose who lack the relevant experience are incompetent thereby as judges of internal goods" (p. 189). One way of discerning such internal goods in any particular case might be to reflect on what those with "the relevant experience" would generally point to as exemplars of excellence and the skills and qualities of character that underpin this—skills and qualities that both contribute to but are also fostered by the practice in question.

External goods, on the other hand, are goods that are contingently attached to a practice by the "accidents of social circumstance" (p. 188)—for example, monetary reward, prestige, status, competitive advantage, and so on. External goods, MacIntyre suggests, are

> characteristically objects of competition in which there must be losers as well as winners. Internal goods are indeed the outcome of competition to excel, but it is characteristic of them that their achievement is a good for the whole community who participate in the practice. So when Turner transformed the seascape in painting or W.G. Grace advanced the art of batting in cricket in a quite new way their achievement enriched the whole relevant community. [pp. 190–191]

One might say the same, closer to home, about Melanie Klein's extension of psychoanalytic technique to work with small children. I shall suggest later that this distinction is important in considering the relation between the enterprise and the organization and its significance for the exercise of leadership.

Putting this aside for the present, it has occurred to me that this concept of a practice adds a useful and in my view necessary adjunct to or expansion of Bion's concept of the work group, which can sometimes appear curiously threadbare: a kind of notional counterpart to basic-assumption functioning. As an Israeli colleague, Joseph Triest, suggested to me in response to an earlier paper, Bion tends to describe work-group mentality in terms of "ego functions, namely coping with reality, in a rational, science-like way". And this can lead to losing sight of the extent to which the work group, as an expression of a practice, may also reflect, and have to contend with and develop through the engagement with, an internal and psychic reality, a reality that is necessarily linked to an internal patterning of object relations around the particular qualities, aspirations, and meanings attached, both consciously and unconsciously, to the nature of the work.

Although Isabel Menzies Lyth does not use the concept of a practice in the way I am drawing on, this extension of Bion's concept of the work group is at least implicit in her studies of nursing (Menzies Lyth, 1988). In effect, she is presenting a concept of the "practice" of nursing. Her focus is on the anxieties aroused internally, not so much by the "practice" as by the total emotional situation that the practice must contain, and then on the ways in which the organization may unconsciously evolve a structure of defence against this. I might say, though, that the problem lies as much in an inadequate formulation or recognition of the practice and its meaning as in the defences elicited by the total work situation: in a lost sense of presence, rather than a present sense of loss.

It is precisely this concept of a practice, I suggest, that is not adequately captured by the idea of primary task, which is both too general and too restrictive to carry this freight of meaning. Recently, Alastair Bain and his colleagues (private communication) in the Australian Institute of Social Analysis coined the term "primary spirit", to refer to "that which breathes life into an organization, the *animating* principle", what gives it psychic resonance. I want provisionally to suggest that the animating principle is linked to MacIntyre's idea of a practice. It is the practice that breathes life into the organization, not the primary task, which I see, rather, as a limiting condition within which a practice is or is required to be framed.

If one defines an enterprise in this way as a "practice", one might say—extending the image—that the organization frames the practice: secures and selects resources; evolves, supports, and maintains requisite structures of activity; creates the conditions under which the "goods and conceptions" internal to the practice can be "realized and extended". This is a central task of management, however distributed management may be, and it includes attention to the limiting conditions bearing on a practice, both internal and external.[3] But equally there is a sense in which the practice may be said to frame the organization, since it is in relation to the practice and its requirements that the organization comes into being.

(There is a caveat I need to enter here: the notions of organization and practice, or organization and enterprise, are not coterminous. Not all practices are organizationally embodied. And any practice is likely to involve and be sustained through cooperative activity that crosses the boundary of any one organization. It is also possible that there are organizations that do not embody a practice, though I am inclined to think that where this is the case, the organization as object will lack inner life, will no longer be felt either to capture or to convey psychic meaning.)

It is here, then, that I want to locate the neglected function of leadership: in the making present of a practice—through example, through formulation, through dialogue, through questioning, through reflection, both internal and with others, and through acts of interpretation.

In an interesting paper, "The Changing Role of the CEO", in the first issue of *Organisational and Social Dynamics*, Edward Shapiro has this to say about the challenge to leadership in a "world of rapid change and little stability":

> In contemporary organisations, the CEO must discern the shape of the institution, articulate and link the inputs of the various stakeholders and forge a clear mission that relates the institution to the larger society . . . must elaborate the institution's place in a world of competition and shape the view others have of it and its function. [Shapiro, 2000, pp. 130–131]

I think this is too single-handed a view of the CEO's role, and indeed Shapiro goes some way later on to meet that objection.

What I want to take from it is the reference to "discernment". Making present a practice is an act of discernment, of bringing into view and articulating what is often tacit—not so much the shape of the institution, but its implicit order: the ways in which it embodies a certain concept or exemplar, or set of concepts and exemplars, around the work it does, the ends and goods intrinsic to this work and the ways in which these inform everything that happens.[4] This is not passive, not a simply scrutiny of what is. It is simultaneously interpretative: a bringing into view of disconnections as well as of connections, of links that seem missing or lost. And, like the interplay of mother and child, it involves acts of exploration and dialogue that are demanding too.

I have been using the present tense here, and in a way this is misleading because I am not talking about something I can readily point to and say "that's what I mean". It's more like, to return to Bion, offering a pre-conception and searching for its realization.

Why then, is this important? I think it is important because without attention to and interpretation of embodied practice, the process of leading and managing change, of "elaborating the institution's place in a world of competition" (or externally driven requirements and challenges), can lose contact with the psychic reality of the organization and risk provoking manic or persecutory responses.

To go back to the paper by Anton Obholzer I cited earlier, he has this to say about the work of managing change (he has been talking about the process of "working through", of coming to terms with and accepting a psychic situation, involving experiences of loss, and the time this may require):

> Any change requires the giving up of something, be it a way of working or a state of self-perception, and the fact that what is being given up might have been only ambivalently valued, as it could be with an ambivalently loved or even hated person, makes no difference to the process of working through and mourning. The same of course also applies to working practices that one had mixed feelings about and that one fights to retain once they become a part of the process of managing change or part of management proposals for change. The core question is thus whether giving up something is an appropriate activity in the service of moving forward on the path of

organisational change, or whether it is an inappropriate, often fashion-determined request for the giving up of something that is best retained as part of the overall institutional culture. Is resistance to giving up something then resistance to change, or is it on-task valuing of tradition? There is no easy answer to this question. No doubt, however, the question needs to be debated—robustly at times—but such a debate has to be held against the backcloth of the primary task, for it is only against that parameter that a true measure of continuity for the organisation, its members, and its products can be reached. [Obholzer, 2001, p. 208]

My only cavil with this statement is its reference to the "backcloth of the primary task". I think, rather, that it is the parameter of the "enterprise", of embodied practice, that may be the true measure of continuity.

Later, Obholzer refers to the various ways in which such organizational debate between leaders and followers can get bogged down in endless forums and reporting back, in which individual and structural responsibility is fudged or disowned. But I think this fudging or disowning is often compounded by the absence of any clear, lively, presented concept of the practice and the ways in which change may bear on it. As a result, I think the accompanying persecutory feelings associated with change can get mis-attributed, so that it becomes difficult to identify the more depressive undertow and what informs it.

It is as if the "practice", the animating spirit, gets hidden—perhaps out of guilt at the extent of one's falling short, or the ambivalence Obholzer refers to, or the uncertainty about one's own or one's group's position and identity in relation to the whole.

Yet I think that it is through bringing the practice into view—discerning it, questioning it, testing it, sorting out what is essential and what are accretions or perhaps defensive distortions—that one may be able to approach change more creatively: to approach it less in terms of the language of loss, the need to "give up something", and more in terms of a language of adaptive development, the "finding of something".

"Practices" are not generally set in stone: they evolve, and indeed the capacity to evolve is built into MacIntyre's definition of a practice, in his reference to the "systematic extension of human powers". This evolution may be generated internally or through some change in the context in which a practice operates and on which it depends.

Consider, for example, the evolution of group relations and its links to the practice of psychological treatment within the Tavistock Clinic. Some time ago, in the context of an assignment during which I had the first anticipations of the territory of this paper, I found myself recalling an episode from Eric Trist's (1985) account of "Working with Bion in the 1940s". At that time, according to Trist,

> the joint Tavistock organization was preparing the Clinic to enter the National Health Service. It would not be permitted simply to give long-term, or even short-term, individual treatment to a few patients. It would have to meet criteria of patient load and economy in the use of scarce professional resources acceptable to a Regional Board. The mission of the Clinic was to pioneer a form of psychotherapeutically orientated outpatient psychiatry appropriate to and acceptable in a National Health Service. It was not just that the queuing problem of patients on the waiting list had to be solved; unless a higher load could be carried with results that could be demonstrated as positive in some degree, the Clinic would not be allowed to continue with its chosen course. The course of psychotherapeutically oriented psychiatry in the National Health Service would be set back. [Trist, 1985, p. 28]

In this postwar context, Trist says, the Tavistock was the only institution entering the National Health Service that was offering outpatient psychological treatment. No one knew what the demand for such treatment would be, but "it was of exceeding importance that the Tavistock as a pioneer should be seen to be reasonably successful in its out-patient mission". Given these considerations,

> in the Adult Department the development of some form of [as yet untried] group treatment seemed the best prospect. Once more Bion was called upon to become the pioneer, though this time many were seen to join him. I remember him putting up a notice: "You can have group treatment now or you can wait a year (or more) and have individual treatment." There were no criteria available for selecting the kinds of patient most likely

> to benefit from treatment in a group. From the earliest appli-
> cants, he started the first group of eight patients who met twice
> a week for sessions of 90 minutes. [p. 29]

The rest is history.

Practices, to return to something I referred to earlier, are (often
if not always) embodied in and sustained by institutions. And
institutions are necessarily concerned with external goods, on
which they depend for their survival and viability. At best the
relation between the institution and the practice is symbiotic, each
informing and sustaining the other. But under the pressures of the
kind of external changes that are now the litany of much of our
political, economic, and social dialogue, this relation can readily
step over into what Bion characterized as "parasitic", whereby
each sucks the life out of the other, the casualty here being the sense
of meaning or organizational identity.

The challenge to leadership I am suggesting is to enable the
organization to work with the tension between the two, between
"practice" and "institution". Too often, I suspect, anxiety associated with this tension is defended against through splitting: between "professionals" and "managers", or between resistors and
resisted. Where this happens, I think it reflects not just the fear of
loss, but the loss of presence: an erosion of or inarticulacy around
the sense of enterprise. Restoring the sense of enterprise is what I
mean by "making present"—in a way that is also demanding, that
challenges and stimulates our inventiveness and our curiosity, and
that invites an engagement from within the practice into its context, the kind of engagement in which the sense of identity is
strong enough to be less fearful of the risk of discovering something new.

Afterword

In the discussion that followed the presentation of this paper, a
number of reservations were voiced around the concept of a "practice", on which it draws.

It might be thought, for example, that I am assuming "practices"—or, rather, those practices that organizations may em-

body—to be self-justifying, in the way that, say, games or painting may be. I am not, however, assuming this. "Practices" that are embodied in organizations typically exist to serve some socially valuable purpose *external* to the practice itself: in the case of farming, the provision of food; in the case of architecture or construction, the design and building of places in which to live, work, worship, and so on; in the case of psychotherapy, the promotion of mental health or the alleviation of mental distress. But these external purposes or goods do not in and by themselves define the practice, nor the internal goods that the practice yields.

As MacIntyre put this point in response to a similar objection:

> The aim internal to such productive crafts [he was using farming and fishing, architecture and construction as examples], when they are in good order, is never only to catch fish, or to produce beef and milk, or to build houses. It is to do so in a manner consonant with the excellences of the craft, so that there is not only a good product, but the craftsman is perfected [or, as I would prefer to say, is enabled to develop] through and in his or her activity. This is what apprentices in a craft have to learn. It is from this that their dignity derives. And it is in terms of this that the virtues [consequent on a practice] receive their initial if partial definition. [MacIntyre, 1994, p. 284]

MacIntyre's use of "productive craft" here needs some qualification. There is no single "productive craft" of farming, fishing, building, psychotherapy, teaching, banking, or whatever. There are many variants, each of which may embody particular forms or ways of practising the "craft", with their own standards of excellence, their own conceptions of internal goods, either implicit or explicit. These variants contribute to forming what might be termed an organization's working identity: the distinctive spirit of its work.

If, for example, I think about my own parent institution, the Tavistock Clinic, the practice it embodies is not captured (contained) simply in the name "psychotherapy". Rather, it involves and draws on a particular cluster of approaches to the work of psychotherapy and associated disciplines, ways of thinking about and responding to emotional disturbance and mental pain, which inform how people talk, relate both to patients and to each other, manage time, handle anxiety, approach referrals, consider evidence, assess outcomes, and so on.

Nor is this "practice" simply a matter of what implicitly or explicitly informs the "productive work" of the organization; it colours and shapes all the surrounding activities on which this work depends. In this sense, what happens between, say, a receptionist and a visitor, client or patient, can be as much an exemplar of a practice as what happens in the consulting-room.

It is just such internal texturing of the work of the organization which the concept of "primary task" both bypasses and eludes. The cost, to my mind, is both to dismantle the expressive meaning attached to the work and to short-circuit, as it were, the creative challenges that externally driven change presents.

Notes

First published in *Organisational and Social Dynamics, 2* (2002): 89–98.

1. In chapter ten, I consider the implications of this observation for the ways we think about and interpret the obtrusion of "basic assumptions" in organizational life.

2. I had read this book when it first appeared but did not then recognize its possible relevance. Eighteen months ago, I came across a reference to it in an inaugural lecture given by John Kay, as director of the Said Business School at Oxford, on "The Role of Business in Society" (Kay, 1998). In this he draws on MacIntyre's formulation to offer a sustained critique of so-called bottom-line definitions of the aims of a business.

3. By "external" limiting conditions, I am referring to questions of demand and supply, changing sociological, economic, and political circumstances, to the things that may challenge the organization's viability in its context. By an "internal" limiting condition, I would include, for example, the psychic costs of the work, its emotional demands, and the anxieties they may arouse.

4. I expand further on this point in the "Afterword" at the end of the paper.

CHAPTER TEN

The work group revisited: reflections on the practice and relevance of group relations

"The Work Group Revisited" was originally presented, in a slightly modified form, to members attending a study weekend in February 2002 at the Tavistock Institute, organized by the Institute's Leadership and Organisation Unit. The title of the weekend was "Reflections on Group Relations, Past Experience and Future Possibilities". Those attending included past members or staff of one or more of the Institute's group relations conferences, together with a small number of interested others.

In the paper, I return to the theme first explored in "Names, Thoughts and Lies" (chapter two): Wilfred Bion's distinction between two modes of mental activity in group life. I argue for a reconsideration of the meaning and significance of the "work group", in both Bion's practice and that of his successors in the field of group relations. I suggest that without such re-thinking, it is not possible either fully to take the measure of the unconscious undertow of group and organizational behaviour or, correspondingly, to make contact with the vitality no less than the defensiveness of our social experience.

It is this "making contact" that, at the end of this particular jour-
ney, may be taken best to represent its direction of travel.

It can be said, I think, without undue exaggeration that the
origin of group relations, as we are familiar with it, both as a
theory and as a method of exploration, is to be found in Wilfred
Bion's distinction between the "work group"[1] and the "basic" or
"basic-assumption" group, where these terms are deployed to capture and define two aspects or modes of mental activity identifiable
within, though not necessarily confined to, all group life.

Whereas, however, the concept of the basic assumptions has
been a continuing focus of attention, curiosity, and puzzlement
both in the literature and in the practice of group relations, that of
the "work group" has, in my view, tended to be taken for granted,
as if it were quite evident and unproblematic. Or as if its role were
simply to get the much more intriguing theme of basic-assumption
functioning off the ground.

I believe this neglect to be a mistake that limits and may sometimes distort both our understanding and our practice. This paper
is my attempt to clarify, deploy, or perhaps simply exorcise this
unease.

Before turning to Bion's characterization of the work group, I
want to emphasize something I alluded to a moment ago. Both of
the two defining terms in Bion's account of experiences in groups
refer to aspects of mental or proto-mental activity (i.e., activity on
the borderline between somatic and psychic life). In this sense,
there is no such thing as a work group or a basic-assumption group
per se; there are only two modes of mental functioning, intrinsic to
all our mental life and always in interplay, just as conscious and
unconscious processes are always in interplay.

Bion regards these two modes of mental functioning as derivatives of what he terms our "inheritance as a group species". On this
view, one might say, our destiny as human animals is from the
outset embedded in the group and subject to its vagaries, whether
or not an actual group is present. As he puts it, in the "Re-View" at
the end of *Experiences in Groups*:

The individual is, and always has been, a member of a group,
even if his membership of it consists of behaving in such a way

that reality is given to an idea that he does not belong to a group at all. The individual is a group animal at war, both with the group and with those aspects of his personality that constitute his "groupishness". . . . In fact no individual, however isolated in time and space, should be regarded as outside a group or lacking in active manifestations of group psychology. [Bion, 1961, pp. 168–169]

Both the work group and the basic group are manifestations of group psychology, and neither, as it were, can escape the clutches of the other. We are fated to experience the tension between the two, here, now, and always. Anything else is an illusion.

Now, I think that one source of difficulty in taking on board the implications of this view, particularly in respect of work-group functioning (and this is a difficulty that Bion's own language occasionally plays into), is that the way such functioning is described makes the work group sound something like a purely intentional object, created for a specific purpose and structured in accordance with rational principles to do with the relation between means and ends.

So, for example, introducing the idea of the work group in the fifth chapter of *Experiences in Groups*, Bion writes:

When a group meets, it meets for a specific task, and in most human activities today co-operation has to be achieved by sophisticated means . . . rules of procedure are adopted; there is usually an established administrative machinery operated by officials who are recognizable as such by the rest of the group, and so on. [p. 98]

He notes that "the capacity for cooperation on this level is great, as anybody's experience of groups will show", and, after differentiating this capacity from what is evident on the basic-assumption level (which he will later refer to as "valency"), continues:

In my experience the psychological structure of the work group is very powerful, and it is noteworthy that it survives with a vitality that would suggest that fears that the work group will be swamped by the emotional states proper to the basic assumptions are quite out of proportion. [p. 98]

Later, he returns to this theme in distinguishing his views from Freud's:

For example, when Freud quotes Le Bon as saying "Groups have never thirsted after truth. They demand illusions and cannot do without them" (Freud, 1921c), I do not feel able to agree with that description. . . . I attribute great force and influence to the work group, which through its concern with reality is compelled to employ the methods of science in no matter how rudimentary a form. I think one of the striking things about a group is that, despite the influence of the basic assumptions, it is the W Group that triumphs in the long run. [pp. 134–135]

In these passages, there is—for me at least—an intriguing and somewhat unsettling shift of tone or register: from dispassionate to passionate, or disengagement to engagement, which is also mirrored in my own response as a reader.

What is it that gives the work group, as sketched in the first sentence I cited, the power, vitality, force, and influence that the subsequent sentences attribute to it?

Following his introduction of the term, Bion distinguishes three elements or ideas in the "mental phenomena" of the work group that are, he says, "linked together . . . just as the emotions in the basic-assumption group appear to be linked together". These are, respectively, the "idea of development" rather than "full equipment by instinct"; the "idea of the value of a rational or scientific approach to a problem" (in however embryonic a form), and also "as an inevitable concomitant of the idea of 'development' [an acceptance of] the validity of learning by experience" (p. 99).

Work-group functioning on this view is a developmental achievement, and in Bion's account, "participation in this activity is possible only to individuals with years of training and a capacity for experience that has permitted them to develop mentally" (p. 143). (I think, incidentally, that this view may be overstated, unless one keeps in mind that the beginnings, at least, of achieved maturity, which is perhaps another way of stating what Bion has in mind, can well predate our conventional views of adulthood.)

How does Bion see the nature of the links he identifies in work-group mentality? It arises out of the work-group's commitment to action, or, as he puts it elsewhere, to "the development of thought designed for translation into action" (p. 145). Because "action inevitably means contact with reality, and contact with reality compels regard for truth and therefore imposes scientific method, and hence the evocation of the work group" (p. 136). Note here the use of the word "evocation", which seems to imply something distinct from just a conscious intent.

In each and every one of these various respects, basic-assumption mentality is, using Bion's formulation, the "dual" of the work group. Here is Bion's description of this "dual" as it emerges in a group of patients:

> In every group it will be common at some time or another to find patients complaining that treatment is long; that they always forget what happened in the previous group; that they do not seem to have learnt anything; and that they do not see, not only what the interpretations have to do with their case, but what the emotional experiences to which I am trying to draw attention can matter to them. They also show, as in psychoanalysis, that they do not have much belief in their capacity for learning by experience—"What we learn from history is that we do not learn from history".
>
> Now all this, and more like it, really boils down to the hatred of a process of development. Even the complaint about time, which seems reasonable enough, is only to complain of one of the essentials of the process of development. There is a hatred of having to learn by experience at all, and lack of faith in the worth of such a kind of learning. A little experience of groups soon shows that this is not simply a negative attitude; the process of development is really being compared with some other state, the nature of which is not immediately apparent. The belief in this other state often shows itself in everyday life, perhaps most clearly in the schoolboy belief in the hero who never does any work and yet is always top of the form— the opposite of the "swot", in fact.
>
> In the group it becomes very clear that this longed-for alternative to the group procedure is really something like arriving fully equipped as an adult fitted by instinct to know without training or development exactly how to live and move and have his being in a group.
>
> There is only kind of group and one kind of man that approximates to this dream, and that is the basic group—the group dominated by one of the three basic assumptions, dependence, pairing, and flight or fight—and the man who is able to sink his identity in the herd. [pp. 88–89]

This is Bion at his most trenchant and provocative. But for me the crux comes in the next sentence:

> I do not suggest for a moment that this ideal corresponds to reality, for, of course, the whole group-therapeutic experience shows that the group and the individuals in it are *hopelessly committed* to a developmental procedure, no matter what might have been the case with our remote ancestors. [pp. 89–90; italics added.]

It is this idea of our being "hopelessly committed to a developmental procedure" that I want to draw attention to, which Bion implies is an attribute not just of the individuals within the group but also of the group as a whole. And doesn't this in turn imply that when earlier Bion has referred to the individual as a "group animal at war, both with the group and with those aspects of his personality that constitutes his 'groupishness'", the term "groupishness" qualifies both work-group and basic-assumption mentality and not just the latter. We are as *driven* to one as to the other.

This is not, I think, just a neat theoretical sleight of hand. For it is this "almost-instinct"[2] quality attached to both aspects of mentality that informs and underlies the intensity of the struggle or conflict that the group and its members are subject to. To put this another way, the *"hatred* of having to learn by experience" would seem redundant unless there were a continuous countervailing pull to learn by experience in the first place. And indeed, it is this countervailing pull that Bion explicitly and paradoxically places as a factor in the extent of the hostility a group can mobilize against any attempt to clarify its tensions. So, for example, describing the psychiatrist's dilemma in a patient group under the sway of basic-assumption dependence, Bion notes:

> It is essential that the psychiatrist should be firm in drawing attention to the reality of the group's claim upon him, no matter how fantastic their elucidation makes those claims appear to be, and then to the reality of the hostility which is aroused by his elucidation.

He then adds:

> It is on occasions such as this that one can see both the strength of the emotions associated with the basic assumptions and the

vigour and vitality which can be mobilized by the work group. It is almost as if human beings were aware of the painful and often fatal consequences of having to act without an adequate grasp of reality, and therefore were aware of the need for truth as a criterion in the evaluation of their findings. [p. 100]

Surely here Bion must mean that it is the unconscious pressure of work-group mentality and the fear this arouses in the dependent group that underscores the hostility to interpretation, just as it is the unconscious processing of work-group mentality that may in time make a difference, may mitigate or bring about a change in the prevailing group functioning, a re-engagement with the *psychic reality* of the task.[3]

From this perspective, the work group is an expression at the group level of a development push (and in the "Re-View" chapter Bion will refer to this as a "compulsion to develop") which is built in to the human organism. Correspondingly, the basic assumptions are an expression of a regressive pull, equally built in, that seeks to evade development and the mental burden or pain that development implies. The tension between this push and pull, which Bion first explored in *Experiences in Groups*, foreshadows and, as it were, recapitulates the story of the individual life that Bion was to spend the rest of *his* life investigating, through the lens of psychoanalytic practice.

To understand what happens in groups—as to understand what happens in the inner world that each of us inhabits—both poles have to be held in view. One might say they are co-dependent, each operating as a silent, unconscious complement to the other.

This point is important because there is sometimes a tendency to construe the distinction between work group and basic group in terms of a differentiation between conscious and unconscious processes. And indeed, Bion's terminology of "sophisticated" and "basic" can play into this, as also can his implicit references to Freud's distinction between primary and secondary processes. (A parallel tendency is to emphasize the emotionality, often qualified by the adjective "primitive", characteristic of basic-assumption functioning, as contrasted with the "rationality" of the work group).

But to go back to something I mentioned at the outset: I think this is to confuse the work group as an intentional object with the work group as an aspect— one might almost say, a *basic* aspect—of human mentality, of which the intentional group is an outcrop. In this guise, the work group exerts an influence on our experience in groups that can be no less unconscious than the basic assumptions. Indeed, I believe that the unconscious life of the group, as of the organization, is always an expression or function of both push and pull. Correspondingly, the task of the consultant is not simply to probe the to-and-fros of the basic assumptions as he or she becomes aware of these but, rather, to probe the reciprocal influence of the two levels of mentality operating within the group and what may be shaping this.

Now, here one comes up against a difficulty that is intrinsic not so much to the theory of group relations, or necessarily to its use as an exploratory tool in applied settings, but, rather, to its institutionalization in group relations conferences and events.

Such conferences, in my view, both open up and simultaneously circumscribe or set limits to what can be explored. Whether or not this circumscription is inevitable—and if it is not, how it can be avoided—I am not sure, and this is a question we can perhaps open up for discussion.

The argument runs as follows:

Group relations conferences, whatever the titles they trade under, are temporary training institutions set up to explore or study the tensions inherent in group life, using a method of experiential learning. This is their manifest intention or "primary task". In order to study these tensions, a frame must be created that mobilizes such tensions from the outset. In part, this frame is created by the very definition of the task, since, as Bob Gosling once put it with characteristic bluntness, "setting up a group that studies its own tensions is a rather peculiar social experience" (Gosling, 1994). This peculiarity is, in turn, considerably compounded by the combination of under- and overdetermination that, appropriately enough, characterizes the organization and structure of the conference and, correspondingly, the behaviour of staff in their work roles. By "underdetermination", I am referring to the stance taken by consultant staff within the "here-and-now" conference events: the refusal to answer questions, to structure the conversation, to address members as individuals, and so on, all of which are aspects of the rejection of basic-assumption leadership.[4] By "overdetermination", I am referring to the firmness, which is often felt to be rigidity, with which boundaries are observed by staff, in particular boundaries of time, which may be taken as the accentuation, almost to the point of caricature, of the work-group culture.

Undue obtrusion of the basic group is precisely what the design of such conferences seeks to sustain and hence make available for exploration. Inevitably, then, attention tends to focus on this level of mental functioning. Correspondingly, the part played by work-group mentality in shaping the tensions that are being experienced can slip out of view. It operates often, I think, as a silent factor, expressed in members' readiness to stay in the field of what can be an extraordinarily unsettling experience and in the ways in which staff—their motives, values, and competences—are continually being tested, including the nature of the authority they exercise and draw on.

I am reminded of Bion's comment, offered in the course of a critique of Freud's views on leadership, that "for reasons I have given, the work-group leader is either harmless through lack of influence with the group, or else a man whose grasp of reality is such that it carries authority" (Bion, 1961, p. 178). It is insofar as staff become aware of doubting their own grasp of reality in this way that they may find evidence of the members' uneasy, ambivalent, but inescapable commitment to development.

Why, then, should this matter? In what sense is this aspect of group relations conferences a limitation? Within the confines of such conferences, perhaps not much. It is, rather, outside these confines, in the application of learning to the dilemmas and challenges of ordinary organizational life, that there is, I think, grounds for caution.

Pierre Turquet used to refer, I believe, talking about the reflective work of staff in group relations events, to "looking for the because clause". What he meant, I think, was to draw a distinction between a formulation of *what* was happening and an interpretation of *why* it was happening. One might think of Bion's discovery of the basic assumptions as derived from his ability and readiness to move from "what is it I am feeling here-and-now" to "why am I feeling it"—a move, incidentally, in which he had, as it were, to problematize what he found himself feeling. Is this feeling some-thing about me that I am importing into this situation, or is it something I am in some way being made to feel? Anyone who has taken staff roles in conferences will be familiar with this move and the difficulties and dangers of making it.

But over and beyond this mental act, there is for us—as perhaps too-knowing followers in Bion's footsteps—another question lying in waiting: Why is this particular dynamic configuration happen-ing now? What is driving the emotional state I am both registering in myself and hypothesizing as a factor in and a function of the group?

To answer this question I believe one has to dig into and, as it were, interrogate the particular quality that attaches to the work-group function: not just the nature of its task but the psychic meaning or meanings that attach to this task and the particular anxieties that this meaning or meanings can arouse. This, of course, is the move that Isabel Menzies Lyth made in her seminal paper on the nursing service of a general hospital, where she showed that the tensions nurses were experiencing in their work arose out of the evolution of an organizational culture in the service of defence against anxieties intrinsic to the nursing task and its psychic mean-ing, which then, as it were, robbed nursing staff of the develop-mental opportunities that that task itself afforded (Menzies, 1960).

Isabel has always acknowledged her debt to Bion's work, and she was herself closely associated with the development of the group relations conference model. But I think she also, in her paper, opened up a vein of thinking that both particularizes and also extends our understanding of the interplay between work-group and basic-group phenomena.

To put this at its sharpest, I would say that, in consultancy work informed by Bion's original differentiation of the two levels of mental functioning, it is the perspective afforded by Isabel's ap-proach that has tended to drive and advance our thinking. That is, in becoming alert to basic group processes in organizational set-tings, we have read these and need to read these as both an expression and as a signal of something unformulated, feared, or evaded that is intrinsic to the nature of the work and its develop-mental challenges and the resonances these evoke in the inner world. Or as something intrinsic to the nature of the relation between that work and its surrounding context. (I am thinking here of the territory that increasingly my own service finds itself in: working with clients who are wrestling with the challenges and fears, both for survival and identity, aroused by the nature and pace of change.)

I believe that it is in these applied situations that we can best test out the practical significance and value of the group relations perspective. Group relations conferences are not an end in themselves, however valuable and deepening we find the experience to be. They are a prelude to application, except that I am not sure "application" is the right word. Perhaps "extension" might be more appropriate.

But the point I want to make here, and which lies behind this suggestion, is that when we move outside the conference territory we find ourselves—or perhaps I should say, we *need* to find ourselves—asking questions, thinking about questions, which the conference itself can seem to bracket out. I mean that we do not often ask ourselves, "What is the nature of the work-group function in conferences; what is its meaning in psychic reality; what fantasies or fears does it arouse in us, and how do these fantasies and fears inform the patterning of basic-assumption (or basic-realm) phenomena, moment by moment?"

Not asking these questions, I think, courts a risk, exacts a cost: the risk and the cost of over-emphasizing the pathological—or, perhaps more accurately, of reading the pathological as if it were a separate, self-contained mental domain, rather than the shadow of development. Or, as a colleague, Branca Pecotic puts it, "a sign that something is moving on" (Pecotic, 2000), the communication of an inner struggle that is at once organizational and personal, the encounter with something not known or known but not formulated, which may certainly repel but may also attract.

I suggested at the start of this paper that within the literature and practice of group relations, the focus of attention, curiosity, and puzzlement has tended to be on the basic assumptions, while the work group has rather been taken for granted. I think now that it may be heuristically useful for a while to reverse this focus: to take basic assumptions for granted—about which we can seem so agile—and take thought afresh about the nature of work-group functioning as this emerges through the hidden, unattended, implicate order of our group and organizational engagements: in dreams, imagery, the flow of feeling, and the signals at once sent and concealed by our shadows.

Notes

An earlier version of the paper was published in *Free Associations, 10* (2003, No. 53): 14–24.

1. You may recall that Bion originally referred to the work group as the "sophisticated group". "Work group" was a term spontaneously introduced by group members, which Bion then co-opted: "The name is short, and expresses well an important aspect of the phenomenon I wish to describe, so that in future I shall use it instead of 'sophisticated group'" (Bion, 1961, p. 98).

2. I have taken this phrase from one of Philip Larkin's poems, "An Arundel Tomb" (1988).

3. Cf. the discussions of this point in *Experiences in Groups*, pp. 71, 118.

4. The impact of this, in Bion's own early practice, is wonderfully well caught in Eric Trist's description of his own experiences as a participant observer in the first of the patient groups that Bion worked with at the Tavistock Clinic: "for weeks on end I remained completely at sea about what he (Bion) was doing though I knew well enough his distinction between group and individual interpretations, his principle of keeping to the former and of concentrating on the group's attitude to himself, etc. In terms of cricket he was letting go by balls I would have expected him to hit and hitting balls I would have expected him to let go by. He was following a pattern unintelligible to me and using a map I did not know" (Trist, 1985, p. 31).

REFERENCES

Alvarez, A. (1999). Frustration and separateness, delight and connectedness: Reflections on the conditions under which bad and good surprises are conducive to learning. *Journal of Child Psychotherapy, 25*: 183–198.

Armstrong, D. (1993). "What Is the Proper Object of a Psychoanalytic Approach to Working with Organisations?" Paper presented at a Scientific Meeting of the Tavistock Centre. (Sound recording available at the Tavistock and Portman NHS Trust Library, the Tavistock Centre, London.)

Armstrong, D. (1998). Thinking aloud: Contributions to three dialogues. In: W. G. Lawrence (Ed.), *Social Dreaming at Work* (pp. 91–106). London: Karnac.

Banet, A. G. (1976). Bion interview. *Group and Organization Studies, 1*: 268–285.

Bateson, G. (1970). Form, substance, and difference. (Nineteenth Annual Korbsybski Memorial Lecture, 9 January 1970.) In: *Steps to an Ecology of Mind* (pp. 448–466). New York: Ballantine Books, 1972.

Bion, W. R. (1957). Differentiation of the psychotic from the non-psychotic personalities. *International Journal of Psycho-Analysis, 38*: 266–275.

Bion, W. R. (1961). *Experiences in Groups and Other Papers*. London: Tavistock. [Reprinted London: Routledge, 1989; London: Brunner-Routledge, 2001.]

Bion, W. R. (1962). *Learning from Experience*. London: Heinemann Medical. [Reprinted London: Karnac, 1984.]

Bion, W. R. (1963). *Elements of Psychoanalysis*. London: Heinemann Medical. [Reprinted London: Karnac, 1984.]

Bion, W. R. (1970). *Attention and Interpretation: A Scientific Approach to Insight in Psycho-Analysis and Groups*. London: Tavistock. [Reprinted London: Karnac, 1984.]

Bion, W. R. (1974). *Brazilian Lectures 2*. Rio de Janeiro: Imago Editora. [Reprinted in: *Brazilian Lectures, 1973 São Paulo; 1974 Rio de Janeiro/São Paulo*. London: Karnac, 1990.]

Bion, W. R. (1976a). Emotional turbulence. In: *Clinical Seminars and Other Works* (pp. 295–305). London: Karnac, 1994.

Bion, W. R. (1976b). On a quotation from Freud. (Paper given at the International Conference on Borderline Disorders, Topeka, Kansas.) In: *Clinical Seminars and Other Works* (pp. 306–311). London: Karnac, 1994.

Bion, W. R. (1979). *The Dawn of Oblivion*. (Book 3 of *A Memoir of the Future*.) Strath Tay, Perthshire: Clunie Press. [Reprinted in: *A Memoir of the Future* (pp. 427–578). London: Karnac, 1991.]

Bion, W. R. (1980). *Bion in New York and São Paulo*. Strath Tay, Perthshire: Clunie Press.

Bion, W. R. (1985). *All My Sins Remembered (Another Part of a Life). The Other Side of Genius (Family Letters)*. Abingdon: Fleetwood Press. [Reprinted London: Karnac, 1991.]

Bion, W. R. (1987a). Making the best of a bad job. In: *Clinical Papers and Four Seminars* (pp. 247–257), ed. F. Bion. Abingdon: Fleetwood Press. [Reprinted London: Karnac, 1994.]

Bion, W. R. (1987b). Evidences. In: *Clinical Papers and Four Seminars* (pp. 239–246), ed. F. Bion. Abingdon: Fleetwood Press. [Reprinted London: Karnac, 1994.]

Bion, W. R. (1990). *Brazilian Lectures: 1973 São Paulo; 1974 Rio de Janeiro/São Paulo*. London: Karnac.

Bion, W. R. (1991). *A Memoir of the Future*. London: Karnac.

Bollas, C. (1987). *The Shadow of the Object: Psychoanalysis of the Unthought Known*. London: Free Association Books.

Bridger, H. (2001). The working conference design. In: G. Amado & A. Ambrose (Eds.), *The Transitional Approach to Change* (pp. 137–160). London: Karnac.

Carr, W. (1996). Learning for leadership. *Leadership and Organization Development Journal, 17* (6): 46–52.

Damasio, A. (2000). *The Feeling of What Happens: Body, Emotion and the Making of Consciousness*. London: Heinemann.

Ellman, R. (1982). *James Joyce* (revised edition). Oxford: Oxford University Press.

Emery, F. E., & Trist, E. L. (1972). *Towards a Social Ecology: Contextual Appreciations of the Future in the Present*. London: Plenum Press.

Forman, M. B. (Ed.) (1931). *The Letters of John Keats*. London: Oxford University Press.

French, R. (2001). "Negative capability": Managing the confusing uncertainties of change. *Journal of Organizational Change Management, 14*: 480–492.

French, R., & Vince, R. (Eds.) (1999). *Group Relations, Management, and Organization*. Oxford: Oxford University Press.

Freud, S. (1917e). Mourning and melancholia. *S.E., 14* (pp. 237–258).

Freud, S. (1921c). *Group Psychology and the Analysis of the Ego. S.E., 18* (pp. 65–144).

Goleman, D. (1998). *Working with Emotional Intelligence*. London: Bloomsbury.

Gosling, R. H. (1979). Another source of conservatism in groups. In: W. G. Lawrence (Ed.), *Exploring Individual and Organizational Boundaries: A Tavistock Open Systems Approach* (pp. 77–86). Chichester: John Wiley. [Reprinted London: Karnac, 1999.]

Gosling, R. H. (1981). A study of very small groups. In: J. S. Grotstein (Ed.), *Do I Dare Disturb the Universe: A Memorial to W.R. Bion* (pp. 633–645). London: Caesura Press. [Reprinted with corrections, London: Karnac, 1983. Also reprinted in: A. D. Colman & M. H. Geller (Eds.), *Group Relations Reader 2* (pp. 151–161). Washington, DC: A. K. Rice Institute, 1985.]

Gosling, R. H. (1994). The everyday work group. In: B. Sievers & D. Armstrong (Eds.), *Discovering Social Meaning: A Festschrift for W. Gordon Lawrence on the Occasion of His 60th Birthday*. Unpublished.

Gosling, R., & Turquet, P. M. (1967). The training of general practitioners. In: R. H. Gosling, D. H. Miller, D. L. Woodhouse, & P. M. Turquet (Eds.), *The Use of Small Groups in Training* (pp. 13–75). Codicote Press & the Tavistock Institute of Medical Psychology.

Gould, L. J., Stapley, L. F., & Stein, M. (Eds.) (2001). *The Systems Psychodynamics of Organizations: Integrating the Group Relations Approach, Psychoanalytic, and Open Systems Perspectives. Contributions in Honor of Eric J. Miller*. London: Karnac.

Hirschhorn, L. (1988). *The Workplace Within: Psychodynamics of Organizational Life*. Cambridge, MA: MIT Press.

Hirschhorn, L. (1997). *Reworking Authority: Leading and Following in the Post-Modern Organization*. Cambridge, MA: MIT Press.

Hirschhorn, L. (1998). *Beyond Anxiety: Passion and the Psychodynamics of Work—Learnings from Lacan*. Philadelphia, PA: Center for Applied Research.

Hirschhorn, L. (1999). The primary risk. *Human Relations, 52*: 5–23.

Huffington, C., Armstrong, D., Halton, W., Hoyle, L., & Pooley, J. (Eds.) (2004). *Working Below the Surface: The Emotional Life of Contemporary Organisations*. London: Karnac.

Hutton, J. (2000). *Working with the Concept of Organisation-in-the-Mind*. London: The Grubb Institute.

Hutton, J., Bazalgette, J., & Reed, B. (1997). Organisation-in-the-mind. In: J. E. Neumann, K. Kellner, & A. Dawson-Shepherd (Eds.), *Developing Organisational Consultancy* (pp. 113–126). London: Routledge.

Jaques, E. (1955). Social systems as a defence against persecutory and depressive anxiety. In: M. Klein, P. Heimann, & R. E. Money-Kyrle (Eds.), *New Directions in Psychoanalysis* (pp. 478–498). London: Tavistock Publications.

Jaques, E. (1989). *Requisite Organization*. Arlington, VA: Cason Hall.

Jaques, E. (1995). Why the psychoanalytical approach to understanding organizations is dysfunctional. *Human Relations, 48*: 343–349, 359–365.

Kay, J. (1998). "The Role of Business in Society." Inaugural Lecture, Said Business School, University of Oxford.

Kets de Vries, M. F. R. (Ed.) (1991). *Organizations on the Couch: Clinical Perspectives on Organizational Behaviour*. San Francisco, CA: Jossey-Bass.

Kirsner, D. (2004). The intellectual Odyssey of Elliott Jaques: From alchemy to science. *Free Associations, 11* (58): 179–204.

Klein, M. (1946). Notes on some schizoid mechanisms. *International Journal of Psycho-Analysis, 27*: 99–110.

Kuhn, T. (1977). *The Essential Tension: Selected Studies in Scientific Tradition and Change*. Chicago, IL: Chicago University Press.

Larkin, P. (1988). An Arundel tomb. In: *Collected Poems*. London: Faber & Faber.

Lawrence, W. G. (1985). Beyond the frames. In: M. Pines (Ed.), *Bion and Group Psychotherapy* (pp. 306–329). London: Routledge & Kegan Paul. [Reprinted in: W. G. Lawrence, *Tongued with Fire: Groups in Experience* (pp. 120–145). London: Karnac, 2000.]

Lawrence, W. G., Bain, A., & Gould, L. J. (1996). The fifth basic assumption. *Free Associations*, 6 (37): 28–55.

MacIntyre, A. (1985). *After Virtue: A Study in Moral Theory* (2nd. edition). London: Duckworth.

MacIntyre, A. (1994). A partial response to my critics. In: J. Horton & S. Mendus (Eds.), *After MacIntyre: Critical Perspectives on the Work of Alasdair MacIntyre* (pp. 283–304). Cambridge: Polity Press.

Meltzer, D. (1968). Terror, persecution and dread. *International Journal of Psycho-Analysis*, 49: 396–401. [Reprinted in: *Sexual States of Mind*. Strath Tay, Perthshire: Clunie Press, 1973, pp. 99–106.]

Meltzer, D. (1992). *The Claustrum: An Investigation of Claustrophobic Phenomena*. Strath Tay, Perthshire: Clunie Press.

Menzies, I. E. P. (1960). A case study in the functioning of social systems as a defence against anxiety. *Human Relations*, 13: 95–121. [Reprinted in: I. Menzies Lyth, *Containing Anxiety in Institutions. Selected Essays, Vol. 1* (pp. 26–44). London: Free Association Books, 1988.]

Menzies Lyth, I. (1988). *Containing Anxiety in Institutions. Selected Essays, Vol. 1*. London: Free Association Books.

Menzies Lyth, I. (1989). A psychoanalytic perspective on social institutions. In: *The Dynamics of the Social. Selected Essays, Vol. 2* (pp. 26–44). London: Free Association Books.

Miller, E. J. (1959). Technology, territory and time: The internal differentiation of complex production systems. *Human Relations*, 12: 243–272.

Miller, E. J. (1993). *From Dependency to Autonomy: Studies in Organization and Change*. London: Free Association Books.

Miller, E. J., & Rice, A. K. (1967). *Systems of Organization*. London: Tavistock Publications.

Neumann, J. E. (1999). Systems psychodynamics in the service of a political organizational change. In: R. French & R. Vince (Eds.), *Group Relations, Management, and Organization* (pp. 54–69). Oxford: Oxford University Press.

Obholzer, A. (2001). The leader, the unconscious, and the management of the organisation. In: L. Gould, L. Stapley, & M. Stein (Eds.), *The Systems Psychodynamics of Organisations: Integrating the Group Relations Approach, Psychoanalytic, and Open Systems. Contributions in Honor of Eric J. Miller* (pp. 197–216). London: Karnac.

Palmer, B. (1986a). "Interpretation and the Consultant Role." Unpublished paper, The Grubb Institute, London.

Palmer, B. (1986b). *Another Decade of Custody? Not If We Can Help It!: The Development of Probation Practice in Cambridgeshire, 1980–1986*. London: The Grubb Institute.

Palmer, B. (2000). In which the Tavistock paradigm is considered as a discursive practice. *Organisational and Social Dynamics, 1*: 8–20.

Palmer, B. (2002). The Tavistock paradigm: Inside, outside and beyond. In: R. D. Hinshelwood & M. Chiesa (Eds.), *Organisations, Anxieties and Defences: Towards a Psychoanalytic Social Psychology* (pp. 158–182). London: Whurr.

Palmer, B., & Evans, C. (1989). Intergroup encounters of a different kind: The experiential research method. *Studies in Higher Education, 17*: 300–301.

Pecotic, B. (2000). "The Tavistock Approach to Group and Institutional Dynamics: A Personal Contribution." Unpublished paper presented at Consulting to Institutions workshop at the Tavistock Clinic.

Reed, B. D. (1976). Organisational role analysis. In: C. L. Cooper (Ed.), *Developing Social Skills in Managers* (pp. 89–102). London: Macmillan.

Reed, B. D. (1982). *Anxiety, Guilt and Authority: Notes on the Place of Supervision in the Structure and Operations of the Probation Service.* London: The Grubb Institute.

Reed, B. D., & Bazalgette, J. (in press). Organisational role analysis at The Grubb Institute of Behavioural Studies: Origins and development. In: J. Newton, S. Long, & B. Sievers (Eds.), *Coaching in Depth: The Organisational Role Analysis Approach.* London: Karnac.

Rice, A. K. (1958). *Productivity and Social Organization: The Ahmedabad Experiment.* London: Tavistock Publications.

Rice, A. K. (1963). *The Enterprise and Its Environment.* London: Tavistock Publications.

Rosenfeld, H. A. (1971). A clinical approach to the psychoanalytic theory of the life and death instincts: An investigation into the aggressive aspects of narcissism. *International Journal of Psycho-Analysis, 52*: 169–178.

Rushdie, S. (1989). *The Satanic Verses.* New York: Viking.

Shapiro, E. R. (2000). The changing role of the CEO. *Organisational and Social Dynamics, 1*: 130–142.

Shapiro, E. R., & Carr, A. W. (1991). *Lost in Familiar Places: Creating New Connections Between the Individual and Society.* New Haven, NJ: Yale University Press.

Simpson, P., French, R., & Harvey, C. E. (2002). Leadership and negative capability. *Human Relations, 55*: 1209–1226.

Steiner, J. (1993). *Psychic Retreats: Pathological Organizations in Psychotic, Neurotic and Borderline Patients.* London: Routledge.

Taylor, D. (1997). Some of Bion's ideas on meaning. *British Journal of Psychotherapy, 14*: 67–76.

Trist, E. (1985). Working with Bion in the 1940s. In: M. Pines (Ed.), *Bion and Group Psychotherapy* (pp. 1–46). London: Routledge & Kegan Paul.

Trist, E. L., & Murray, H. (Eds.) (1990). *The Social Engagement of Social Science: A Tavistock Anthology, Vol. 1: The Socio-Psychological Perspective*. London: Free Association Books.

van Reekum, G. (2004). "On a Quotation from Bion." Paper presented at the Annual Symposium of the International Society for the Psychoanalytic Study of Organizations, Coesfeld, Germany.

Wright, K. (1991). *Vision and Separation*. London: Free Association Books.

INDEX

accountability, 7, 47, 95, 98, 102
    relations, 95, 98
    fluid, within organization
        [case example], 93–100
aim, 7, 50, 138
Alvarez, A., 124–128
anxiety(ies), 53, 70, 80, 84, 107, 131,
        148
    case examples, 38, 48
    containment of, 51, 83, 126, 129,
        138
        illusory, 77, 78
        by organization, 76, 79
    defence against, 65
        social systems as, 101, 104, 105
    developmental, and psychic
        retreat, 85–86
    individual, 72, 77, 127
    institutional, and splitting, 136
    paranoid–schizoid, 70, 74
    psychotic, 101
area, transitional, 86
Australian Institute of Social
        Analysis, 131

authority, 7, 43, 98, 147
    delegation of, 84–85
    devolution of, 38
autism, childhood, 126

Bain, A., 78, 86, 131
Balint, M., 111–112
    groups, 119, 123
Banet, A. G., 26
basic assumption(s) [Bion], 3, 6, 12,
        54, 78, 138
    dependence, 13, 23, 32, 91, 114,
        143, 144
    fight–flight, 13, 23, 32, 91, 114,
        143
    functioning, 131, 140, 145
        vs. work group functioning,
            65, 77, 91, 121, 144, 148
    group vs. work group, 32, 140–
        150
    guilt as, 23
    leadership, 147
    me-ness, 86–89
    mentality, 143

basic assumption(s) (*continued*):
  mobilization of, 23–24
  pairing, 13, 23, 32, 91, 114, 143
  phenomena, 149
Bateson, G., 42
Bavelas, A., 112
Bazalgette, J., 4, 23, 33
beta-elements [Bion], 74
Bion, W. R., 2, 65, 68, 72, 92, 112, 114,
      116, 133, 136, 139
  basic assumptions, *see* basic
      assumption(s)
  beta-elements, 74
  "bizarre objects", 74
  "catastrophic change", 57
  container/contained, 31, 108, 110
  emotional experience in work
      with groups, 31–33
  on existence vs. meaning, 67
  group(s):
    experiences in, 10–28
    mentality, 77, 81, 91, 100
    work at Tavistock, 135
  interventions/interpretations of,
      14–15
  knowledge, 13
  learning, genesis of, 127
  lies, 13, 19–20
  linking, 17
  meaning/understanding, 60
  names/naming, 13
  "O"/ultimate reality, 15
  paranoid–schizoid and
      depressive positions, 78
  pathological splitting, 74
  projective identification, 78
  psychotic processes, 75
  "reversible perspective", 45
  "shadow of the future cast
      before", 57
  "sophisticated group", 150
  thoughts/thinking:
    "thinking under fire", 61
    "thoughts in search of a
        thinker", 51
  transformation, 15–17

"work group", 14, 131
  vs. basic-assumption
      mentality, 91, 140–150
  institutionalized, 26–27
  mentality, 131
"bizarre objects" [Bion], 74
Bollas, C., 44, 51, 64
boundary(ies), 3, 92
  conditions, of organization, 46,
      52, 90, 93, 103–104, 109
  group, as barrier, 22
  individual, 13, 59
    as barrier, 22
  defence of, 19, 32
  internal/external, 10–28
  names/naming as, 13
  organizational, 6, 132
    relaxation of, 83, 99
  school, 33
  permeability of, 6
  role, 6, 97
    blurring of, 98
  self/other, 10–28
  structural, 6, 106
  task, 83
    and omnipotence, 121, 122
  technology, 83
  territory, 83
  time, 83, 147
Bridger, H., 87, 106

Carr, W., 3–4, 9
case examples:
  absence of passion in mental
      health trust, 107–108
  emotional constellation in
      multinational investment
      bank, 93–100
  management of vulnerability in
      hospital setting, 46–51
  organization-in-the-mind:
    in residential community
        setting, 36–43
    in school setting, 33–36
  organizations, psychic retreat
      faced by, 85–89

recovery of meaning:
  in college of further education,
    61–64
  de-centredness in student
    counselling in university,
    58–61
  Working Conference Training
    Group [Gosling], 117–118
"catastrophic change", 19, 20, 57
categorization, 104
Cézanne, P., 16
"chambermade music" [Joyce], 91,
    103
change, 53, 54, 59, 62, 67
  catastrophic, 19, 20, 57
  and continuity, 34
  cultural, 44
  externally driven, 37, 138
    global, 20, 67, 68, 71, 82, 83,
      132, 136, 149
  human costs of, 89
  and identity, 126, 134, 136
  managing, 133–134
  organizational, 47, 134
  in primary task, 128
  resistance to, 47, 50, 109, 119, 120,
    128, 134
  structural, 37, 106
  "transformational", 83
Children Act, 37
Clausewitz, C. P. G. von, 13
client(s), 6
  perspective of, 53–54
community in transition, letting go
    [case example], 36–43
consultancy (passim):
  psychoanalytically informed
    approach to, 65
container/containment, 26, 47–48,
    76–77, 84, 106
  and contained [Bion], 31, 108, 110
    interplay between, 66
  illusory [Steiner], 78, 80, 81
  for meaning, dream as, 55, 64
context of organization, 6
"core values", 66, 83

countertransference, 2, 8, 12, 45, 53,
    59
creativity, 83, 108, 122, 128
culture:
  "of openness" [Hirschhorn], 83
  of organization, 6
  and organization and structure,
    interrelations between, 32

Damasio, A., 91
"de-centredness", 59–61
defence(s):
  mechanism:
    institutional, 50
    psychic, 105
  and resistances, 36
  strategies of, organizational, 93
defensive organization(s) [Steiner],
    72
"de-layering", 66
denial, strategies of, organizational,
    93
dependence, 13, 23, 32, 91, 114, 143
"dependent self" and internal
    organization, 75
depersonalization, 84, 104
depressive position, 70, 74, 78
Descartes, R., 19
"desire" vs. mental "flow"
    [Hirschhorn], 82
destructiveness, primitive, 72
development vs. survival, 28, 67,
    89, 128
Dilke, C., 27
"downsizing", 66
dream(s)/dreaming, 25, 27, 143,
    150
  and meaning, 64
  and psychic retreats, 76
  and recovery of meaning [case
    example], 63–64
  in role consultation, 55
  social, 44

Ellman, R., 110
Emery, F. E., 57

emotion(s) in organizations, 90–110
    investment bank [case example],
        93–100
emotional experience, 35–39, 42,
        110
    of analytic couple, 52
    and context, 31–33
    group, 20–23, 52
        Bion, 143
    of individual, 52
    within organization, 6
    and names/naming, 16
    in organization, 6, 9, 53, 104
        as bounded entity, 6
        patterning of, 103
        and questions of identity, 107
        significance of, 101
    in psychoanalysis, 30
    and thought/thinking, 10–28
        transformation of [Bion], 15, 16
    in work with organizations, 5–6,
        56, 64, 102, 105, 109
    object of, 49–54
    and psychoanalysis, link
        between, 29–43
"emotional intelligence", 90–110
enactment, 5, 75, 80, 101, 105, 125
    vs. in-actment, 69
    of oedipal phantasies, 97, 99
"endeavour" [McIntyre], 129–131
enterprise, 103, 125, 134, 136
    "form of activity" [MacIntyre],
        108–110
    vs. organization, 54, 108–109, 129,
        130, 132
    "requisite structure" of [Jaques],
        82
environment(s):
    of organization, 6
    turbulent, theory of [Emery &
        Trist], 57
"essential tension", 25–27
Evans, C., 25
experience, emotional: *see*
    emotional experience

fight–flight, 13, 23, 32, 91, 114, 143
"form of activity" [MacIntyre], 108
Forman, M. B., 28
fragmentation, primitive states of,
        77
French, R., 28, 55, 68, 129
frequency, contracted, 7
Freud, S., 30, 54, 116, 127, 141–142,
        147
    primary and secondary
        processes, 145
    "shadow of the object that fell
        upon the ego", 57, 61–64
Fulbourn Scholarship, 112

Goleman, D., 110
Gosling, R. H., 13, 111–123, 146
Gould, L. J., 2, 78, 86
Grace, W. G., 130
group(s):
    experiences in, 18–20
    and thought/thinking, 20
    understanding [Bion], 10–28
    leader, role of, 123, 147
    mentality [Bion], 32, 77
    relations:
        conference(s), 13, 19, 20, 25,
            100, 111, 114, 139, 146–149
        Institutional Event, 3, 79
        work group, 139–150
        transitional state of mind in, 121–
            122
Grubb Institute, xv, 2, 3, 9, 10, 22, 23,
        27, 29, 33, 36, 46, 79
guilt, 23, 76, 77, 84
    as basic assumption, 23
    persecutory, 23

Halton, W., 90, 110
Harvey, C. E., 28
Hirschhorn, L., 7, 34, 81, 82, 83, 84
Horowitz, S., 110
hospital, primary process of, 50
Hoyle, L., 90, 110
Huffington, C., 90, 110

Hutton, J., 4, 9, 29

identity:
    organizational, 129, 136
    vs. survival, 108–109, 149
in-actment, 5, 100, 101, 105
    vs. *en*actment, 69
Institute of Psychoanalysis, 29
institution(s):
    in the mind (*passim*):
        vs. organization in the mind, 4,
        9
    transformations in, 25–27
    work with, and psychoanalysis,
        29–43
Institutional Event, in group
    relations conferences, 3, 79
internal and external goods, 130–
    136
internal organization, Steiner's
    concept of, 69, 72, 75, 80
International Society for the
    Psychoanalytic Study of
    Organizations, 44
interpersonal space, 52, 54
intrapsychic meaning, 63
intrauterine life, development of
    personality during, 17

Jaques, E., 9, 82, 98, 101–105
Joyce, J., 91, 92

Kay, J., 138
Keats, J., "negative capability", 27–
    28
Kets de Vries, M. F. R., 9
"key performance indicators", 66
King, P., 13
Kirsner, D., 9
Klein, M., 11, 30, 31, 66, 72, 73, 116,
    120, 127, 130
Kraemer, S., 122
Kuhn, T., 27

Larkin, P., 150

Lawrence, W. G., 44, 53, 78, 86, 128
leadership:
    basic-assumption, 147
    relevance of, 124–136
learning, 22, 62, 68, 83, 87, 117, 126,
    146, 147
    "conference", 118
    by experience, 142–144
    experiential, 119
    genesis of, 127
    paradox of, 118
    within transitional space, 120
Le Bon, G., 142
Leicester Conference, 115, 118
lie(s), 13, 19–21, 23–24, 119
    true, 19
linking, resistance to, 17
loss, intolerance of, 70

MacIntyre, A., 108
    definition of practice, 129–131,
        134
    productive crafts, 137–138
Macmillan, H., 28
meaning, 4, 15, 22, 23, 30, 42, 51, 97,
    106, 109, 131, 138
    Bion's ideas on, 60
    as concern of psychoanalysis
        [Rycroft], 65
    and dreams/dreaming, 64
    intrapsychic, 63
    "management of", postmodern,
        66
    organizational, 52, 60, 61, 69–89,
        93, 136
    psychic, 132, 148
    recovery of, 55–68
        in university student
            counselling service [case
            example, 58–61
        Taylor's ideas on, 60–61, 65
    meetings, ritualization of, 83–84
Meltzer, D., 76, 89
me-ness (baM), basic-assumption,
    86–89

mental "flow" vs. "desire"
    [Hirschhorn], 82
mental functioning, 148
mental space, 14
Menzies, I. E. P., *see* Menzies Lyth
Menzies Lyth, I., 9, 13, 31, 65, 79–81,
    101, 104–105, 131, 148
Miller, E. J., 52, 106, 111, 120, 128
"mission", 66
mourn, inability to, 70
Murray, H., 2

name(s)/naming, 42
    as boundary, 13
    defensive use of, 22–23
    and the lie, 23
    and lies, 24
    the unnameable, 16
National Health Service, 135
"negative capability" [Keats], 27–
    28
Neumann, J. E., 2

"O"/ultimate reality [Bion], 15
Obholzer, A., xv–xvii, 125, 128, 133,
    134
object(s):
    analytic, in organizational work,
        emotional experience as,
        44–54
    organization as, 103–104, 109
    relatedness, 127
    transitional, 86–89
omnipotence, 26, 120, 121, 122
open systems theory, 2, 45, 50, 82,
    106, 118, 128
organization(s) (*passim*):
    "ambience" of [Menzies Lyth],
        81
    emotions in, 90–110
    vs. enterprise, 54, 108–109, 129,
        130, 132
    in the mind, ix, 3–4, 6–9, 47, 52–
        54, 77–85
    vs. institution-in-the-mind, 9

    as working tool in
        organizational consultancy,
        29–43
    as object, 109
    boundary conditions of, 103–
        104
    pathological, 71, 81–82
    Steiner's ideas on, 72–77
    post-modern, 83
    as process, 104–106
    psychic retreat faced by [case
        example], 85–89
    Steiner's formulation of, 79
    as structure, 104–106
    and culture, interrelations
        between, 32
Organisation for Promoting
    Understanding of Society,
    124
organizational dynamic(s), 5, 71
organizational identity, 129, 136
organizational meaning, 60, 61, 69
organizational object, 103, 104, 128,
    129
organizational role analysis, 33, 38
organizational work, analytic object
    in, 44–54
    emotional experience as, 52–54

pairing, 13, 23, 32, 91, 114, 143
Palmer, B., 12, 23, 25, 82
paranoid–schizoid anxiety, 74
paranoid–schizoid position, 70, 78
pathological organization, 71, 81, 82
    Steiner's ideas on, 72–77
Pecotic, B., 125, 126, 149
persecution, primitive states of, 77
persecutory guilt, 23
personality, development of during
    intrauterine life, 17
"personalized" organization vs.
    "organization-in-the-mind",
    77–85
phenomena, transitional, 40, 119
Pooley, J., 90, 110

"post-modern organization", 83
postmodern theories, 66
power, 7
    politics, 117
primary objects, 66
primary process:
    of institution, 50, 52
    vs. primary task, 45–54
    vs. secondary process [Freud], 54,
        145
"primary risk" [Hirschhorn], 82
"primary spirit" [Bain], 131
primary task, 28, 34, 128–131, 134,
        138, 146
    vs. primary process, 44
primitive destructiveness, 72, 80
process, organization as, 104–106
    see also primary process
"productive craft" [MacIntyre], 137
Profumo, J., 13, 28
projection(s), 76, 80
    in organizations, members', 3, 4,
        50–51
    processes of, organizational, 5
    and projective identification, 72–
        73
    strategies of, organizational, 93
projective identification, 72–73, 75,
        78
    institutional, 49
    primitive, 74
"psychic costs" [Hirschhorn], 83
psychic meaning, 132, 148
psychic reality, 30, 67, 131, 145, 149
    of organization, 99, 133
"psychic retreats" [Steiner], 69–89
psychoanalysis, applied, 3, 30

recovery of meaning, 55–68
    de-centredness in university
        student counselling service
        [case example], 58–61
    dream material in college of
        further education [case
        example], 61–64

Reed, B., 4, 9, 23, 33
"requisite structure" of enterprise
        [Jaques], 82
resistance(s):
    and defences, 36
    and transformations, 17–20
reversible perspective, 45
"re-visioning", 83
Rice, A. K., 11–12, 100, 106, 111, 114,
        120, 128
role consultation, 2, 4
    dream material in, 55
Rosenfeld, H. A., 76
Rushdie, S., 16, 20, 28
Rycroft, C., 65

Said Business School, Oxford, 138
schools, work in, 22–23
secondary process vs. primary
        process [Freud], 54
self:
    and object, interplay between, 66
    sense of, and symbol formation,
        40–41
separation:
    achievement of, 42–43
    intolerance of, 70
"serious play" [Palmer & Evans], 25
Shapiro, E. R., 3–4, 132–133
Simpson, P., 28
social dreaming, 44
"sophisticated group" [Bion], 150
space(s):
    contracted, 7
    interpersonal, 52
        bounded, 54
    mental, 14
    transitional, 86–89, 119, 120–121
splitting, 72, 76, 80, 89, 101, 109, 136
    "normal processes of", 73–74
    pathological, 74–75
Stapley, L. F., 2
Stein, M., 2
Steiner, J., "psychic retreats", 69–89
Stokes, J., 53, 60

structure:
    organization as, 104–106
    of organization, 6
    and organization and culture,
        interrelations between, 32
    survival, 68, 107, 136
    vs. development, 28, 67, 89, 128
    vs. identity, 108, 109, 149
    symbol formation, and sense of self,
        40–41
    system psychodynamics, 2
    systems theory, open, 2, 45, 50, 82,
        106, 118, 128

task, 7, 25, 28, 34, 42, 44, 49, 50
    boundaries of, 83, 98
    as boundary condition of
        organization [Miller], 52
    double, in working conferences
        [Bridger], 87
    of organization, 6, 79, 81, 103
        primary, 128
    primary, 128–131, 134, 138, 146
    of work group, 25
Tavistock:
    Centre, 5
    Clinic, 2, 5, 29, 60, 70, 104, 111–
        116, 124–126, 135, 137, 150
    Consultancy Service, xv, 2, 83, 87,
        90, 110
    Institute of Human Relations, 2,
        5, 11–12, 25, 104–106, 112–
        113, 128, 139
    paradigm in organizational
        consultancy, 82
    tradition, 2
Taylor, D., 60–61, 65–66
technology:
    as boundary condition of
        organization [Miller], 52
    boundaries of, 83
territory:
    as boundary condition of
        organization [Miller], 52
    boundaries of, 83

theory of turbulent environments
    [Emery & Trist], 57
thing-in-itself [Bion], 15, 28
"third ear" [Stokes], 53
thought(s)/thinking, xvi, 10–28
    and the group, 20–23
    and lies, 19
    realization of, 36
    "in search of a thinker" [Bion],
        51
    unthought, 27
time:
    as boundary condition of
        organization [Miller], 52
    boundaries of, 83
    contracted, 7
    "real" vs. illusory timelessness,
        48
timelessness, illusory, vs. "real"
    time, 48
transference, 2, 8, 12, 30, 34, 45, 53,
    59, 96
transformation(s):
    arena for, work group as, 15–17,
        24–25
    in institutions, 25–27
    and resistances, 17–20
"transformational change", 83
transitional area, 86
transitional objects, 86–89
transitional phenomena, 40, 119
transitional space, 86–89, 119, 120,
    121
Triest, J., 131
Trist, E. L., 2, 12, 57, 106, 113–114,
    135–136, 150
Trotter, W., 17
Turquet, P. M., 3, 13, 79, 123, 147

ultimate reality/"O" [Bion], 15
understanding, Bion's ideas on, 60
"unthought known" [Bollas], 51, 52,
    64
unthought thought, negative
    capability, 27

value(s), 4, 22, 67, 147
  core, 66, 83
van Reekum, G., 57
Vince, R., 55, 68
"vision", 66
vulnerability, management of, in
    hospital setting [case study],
    46–51

Weiskrantz, L., 112
Whole System Meetings, 87
William Alanson White Institute,
    New York, 44
Winnicott, D. W., 40, 63, 86, 119
Wisdom, J., 14
withdrawal, strategies of,
    organizational, 93
work group, 23, 25–26, 131

as arena for transformations, 15–
    17, 24–25
and basic-assumption group, 32
functioning [Bion], 14, 24–25, 131,
    139–150
  vs. basic-assumption
    functioning, 65, 77, 91, 121,
    144, 148
  in conferences, 149
institutionalized [Bion], 26
"mental phenomena" of, 142–143
and task, 25
"workplace within" [Hirschhorn],
    7, 8, 34
Wright, K., 40

Zangwill, O., 113
zone, transitional, 119